CHANNELING
INTO THE NEW AGE

CHANNELING
INTO THE NEW AGE

The "Teachings" of Shirley MacLaine and Other Such Gurus

AN UNAUTHORIZED ACCOUNT

BY HENRY GORDON
Foreword by Isaac Asimov

PROMETHEUS BOOKS
Buffalo, New York

91 90 89 88   4 3 2 1

Library of Congress Card Catalog Number: 88-043041
ISBN 0-8975-462-1

This book is dedicated neither to the believers nor to the skeptics, but to those who do not know what to believe and are looking for explanations.

Contents

Foreword 9

Acknowledgments 13

Introduction 15

PART ONE

The New Age 21
The Channelers 75
Shirley MacLaine 107

PART TWO: The "Teachings"

Philosophical "Teachings" 133
Metaphysical "Teachings" 149
Scientific "Teachings" 177

Epilogue 195

Selected Bibliography 197

Foreword

The Will to Believe
by Isaac Asimov

I was picked up by a taxi the other day, and the driver made it quite plain that he recognized me and liked my books. This is quite flattering, of course, and made it difficult for me to disagree with him when he turned out to be one of those opinionated drivers who inflict their views on their helpless fares.

It seemed that since I was a science-fiction writer he assumed that I automatically believed every wretched piece of lunacy propagated by the sly and the ignorant.

One by one, he trotted out his beliefs—in flying saucers, in Sasquatch and the Loch Ness Monster, in pyramid power, in the New Age gibberish, and so on. In every case, he would pause and say, very earnestly, "All this is well documented."

My only concern, of course, was whether his driving was saner than his views, so I didn't bother asking him what he meant by "well documented." I suspect that what he meant was that some knave had said so. For instance, if someone writes a book describing in detail his kidnapping by a flying saucer, that book becomes a "document" and the incident is therefore "well documented."

Ought I to have argued with him?

No! First, because a New York taxi driver holds your life in his hands and it would not be wise to upset him. Second, because it would have done no good.

All history shows that even more powerful than the instinct of self-preservation is the will to believe. A selfless human being is rare, but a skeptical human being seems to me to be even rarer.

Why is this? In my opinion there are some beliefs that most individuals *must* have if they are to face life with even a minimum of success. An individual *must* believe he (or she) is strong and capable. Since this is almost invariably not so and since life is constantly proving it, the individual must transfer his ego to a larger group: a family, a gang, a nation, and then he (as part of the whole) *is* strong and capable. To maintain that view, he will proceed to believe any fable that strengthens it and denounce anything, however truthful, however obvious, that would tend to weaken it. (And so people involve themselves enthusiastically with family feuds, gang rumbles, riots, and wars.)

Again, in an uncertain world, with terror and disaster lurking unseen in the mirk of the future; with misfortune ready to spring upon you in the very next moment; life would be unbearable if you could not find some way of easing matters—of being warned about the existence of specific monsters ahead, and how to thwart them. Why else would we turn to astrologers, palm-readers, dream-analyzers, fortune-tellers, and every other variety of palpable quack and enrich them in return for their phony advice. Nothing will wean the future-frightened public from them, for the belief seems universal that a false security is better than none.

Finally, there is the absolute refusal to accept the fact of death. We are the only species we know of, now or ever, that has discovered that death is inevitable for every individual.

In reaction, the vast majority of us simply deny that death is death, and fervently believe in ghosts, in spirit worlds, in an afterlife, in the transmigration of souls. The evidence in favor of immortality of any part of ourselves is absolutely zero, but the will to believe easily overcomes that little matter.

Hence we have the incredible nonsense dished up, without shame, by the likes of Shirley MacLaine; all of it "well documented" simply because she says so.

And here we have Henry Gordon writing a book that considers the MacLaine nonsense and debunks it.

Will this harm MacLaine? I doubt it. Will it win away the helpless innocents who pant after her gibberish? I doubt it.

Then why bother?

First, there's a matter of self-respect. If one is fortunate enough to be gifted with a modicum of rationality, he (or she) has the responsibility to use it, even if the matter seems hopeless. If one has the rare ability to be able to say, "But there's no real evidence for this and it doesn't seem to have any rational meaning," then he is required to say so as loudly and as forcefully as he can.

Second, he may persuade *some* waverers; he may add, by however little, to the total sum of rationality in the world. And that he is bound to do, for the good of all of us, and as his reason for living.

Acknowledgments

I would be remiss if I did not express my appreciation to the historians of conjuring and of the occult who have recorded the remarkable meanderings of these arts over the centuries.

Neither can I neglect to mention my supportive and patient mate, Zita Shirley, who cajoles, cautions, urges on, endures, and proofreads.

The support and the provision of priceless information by Barry Karr, on the staff of the Committee for the Scientific Investigation of Claims of the Paranormal, is greatly appreciated. Likewise appreciated is the information gleaned from the newsletters of the various skeptical groups associated with CSICOP, such as the Bay Area Skeptics, the British Columbia Skeptics, and the Rocky Mountain Skeptics. A tip of my hat, too, to the National Council Against Health Fraud.

And finally, my sincere thanks to Shirley MacLaine and other such gurus. Without their profound and remarkable observations this book would not exist.

Introduction

The only reason, it seems to me, to write a book, is to have something to say. Well, Shirley MacLaine has had lots to say—and she's still saying it.

So I thought it only fair for me to say something about what she is saying, and has said. What I have to say is certainly in a more condensed form than Shirley's sayings. But I feel I have said all I have to say about what MacLaine has been saying. To say more would be superfluous—it says here.

If you think what I have just written is slightly obtuse, try reading some of Shirley's books. On second thought, don't —at least not until you have finished this book and are in a better position to decide whether to risk your hard-earned cash on a collection of nonsense that is having a profound influence on more people than you can imagine.

My original thought was to write a book devoted strictly to the "teachings." But it occurred to me that to concentrate only on the "teachings" would be to provide them out of context. The uninformed reader would not be able to relate them to the New Age scene as it exists today.

This resulted in the book you are now holding. In the first chapter I have attempted to provide a thorough analysis of what "New Age" means, its derivations and its content, the type of people involved in it, the forces that motivate it and prolong it, and the many dangers it presents.

The second chapter deals with the spirit mediums of the past, their methods of operation, and the channelers of the New Age, who now dominate the scene.

One must recognize the changes in terminology. Fortune tellers have become known, in this modern era, as "psychics." Psychics evolved into psychic advisers. Even psychic advisers are falling out of fashion. They are evolving into "channelers."

This calls for further explanation. Originally, a "channeler" was an updated version of a spirit medium. If you attended a seance, the medium professed to making contact with a "control," a spirit entity with whom previous contact was already established. Every medium had a favorite and regular control. The control would then make contact with a deceased relative or friend of the client and relay messages back and forth—much like a translator at the United Nations.

In this New Age, the channelers are off on a new kick. Instead of getting in touch with relatives who have "passed over" they now contact ancient entities that inhabited this earth thousands of years ago. These prehistoric sages dispense advice to the anxiety-ridden people who eagerly pad the bank accounts of the channelers. So what we have now are dinosauric Dear Abbys dishing out deceptive and devious divinations to the duped.

The third chapter, on the mystical and marvelous Shirley MacLaine, is a brief biography of a career that descended from the sublime to the ridiculous—and rose to literary and financial heights. Her imagination soars higher than the astral plane!

The "teachings" are divided into three separate categories. Philosophical "teachings" are those I felt expressed MacLaine's philosophy on various subjects. Metaphysical "teachings," of course, are her pronouncements on the mystical and the paranormal. Scientific "teachings" are her educational gems, which will round out our intellects and enrich our lives.

I have made an earnest effort to offer what I think is a fair comment on each and every pronouncement. But you must realize it has not been easy to interpret the meaning of some of Shirley's statements. If I have erred in any of the interpretations, I ask the forgiveness of the reader, and of Miss MacLaine.

It will be charged by some that the statements are taken out of context. Indeed they had to be, but I believe they stand on their own. And I have been careful to attribute each and every one to its source.

PART ONE

The New Age

Ask ten sociologists for a definition of the New Age movement, and you may get ten different answers. *Today* it appears to be a reversion to "personal spirituality" outside the parameters of traditional religion. It developed out of the human-potential movement, itself a product of the "me" generation.

The New Age encompasses the entire field of the paranormal and all the irrational beliefs associated with it. This smorgasbord includes yoga, mysticism, astrology, acupuncture, chiropractic, nature cults, hypnosis, herbal medicine, Jungian psychology, dietary therapy, meditation, faith healing, telepathy, psychokinesis, spiritualism, clairvoyance, biofeedback, biorhythms, reincarnation, and all sorts of psychological techniques for "heightened awareness."

When I emphasize *today,* I mean that, although these practices have existed for many years, a new element has been added.

We have always had psychics, mediums, fortune-tellers, prognosticators, astrologers, health-food addicts, alternative medicine, the self-absorbed, and the faddists who adopt every way-out innovation. The big difference is that now the major publishing houses have got into the act in a big way. And many top entertainment personalities have joined them in hawking their questionable wares.

In addition, we now have well-heeled networks with a vested interest in promoting all this nonsense.

The motivation for the New Age movement is revealed in Marilyn Ferguson's landmark book, *The Aquarian Conspiracy,* which was first published in 1980 and has now been re-released in a revised, updated edition. The California-based author is more active than ever, conducting seminars, appearing on radio and television talk-shows, and editing and publishing the *Brain/Mind Bulletin.* When she wrote this bible of the New Age movement, it is doubtful that she or the publishers anticipated its impact on the social scene.

Why did Ferguson choose the title *The Aquarian Conspiracy?* The developing movement, she explains, was composed of people and groups who were not only co-operating, but were in collusion—hence they were *conspiring.* And she called it "Aquarian" because we were entering the astrological age of Aquarius, "a millennium of love and light."

Those who scoff at the warnings about the potential effects of the New Age movement should read the author's opening remarks. She writes of a leaderless but powerful network working to bring about radical changes in society and to break with certain elements of Western thought. Indeed, this is exactly what is happening today—the swing toward Eastern mystical philosophies and away from "rational thinking." Ferguson details her concept of how New Age thought should and would affect politics, science, health services, education— the whole structure of Western society.

One cannot argue with all her ideas. In education, for example, she compares present teaching methods with the projected new ones. Her emphasis on asking good questions, having access to information, the teaching of certain subjects in new ways, using experiment and experience in and out of the classroom—all these are not likely to be controversial. But when she advocates the teaching of self-imagery and inner experience she is venturing into murky territory.

This is just one example of how New Age advocates spread their teachings. They promote the basically good qualities of personal behavior with which no one can argue, but at the same time claim beneficial effects from all kinds of paranormal, irrational nonsense that can be so harmful to so many.

Ferguson writes, as do most paranormalist authors, about the power of intuition. It can be extended, she says, from the individual to a group. "Groups of the Aquarian Conspiracy," she writes, "often listen for inward guidance. . . . Rather than charting their activities exclusively by logic, they seek a kind of consensual intuition." The message is clear: Logical thinking is not dependable.

On the subject of science, she quotes several physicists who have theories that border on the mystical. At the same time she quotes statements, taken out of context, attributed to such great scientists as John Wheeler, Niels Bohr, and Albert Einstein. These quotations are presented as supporting the case for the paranormal, but in their proper context they most definitely do not.

Many of the statements of Shirley MacLaine cited later in this book may well have been inspired by Marilyn Ferguson's writings.

A reader of *The Aquarian Conspiracy*, not knowing his background, might seriously consider Fritjof Capra's remark, "The 1980s will be a revolutionary time, because the whole structure of our society does not correspond with the worldview of emerging scientific thought." Capra is the author of *The Tao of Physics* (1975), and a strong supporter of the merging of theoretical physics with Eastern mystical philosophy—a murky hodge-podge of pseudoscientific theories sure to influence the unsophisticated student.

Biologist Lyall Watson is quoted several times in Ferguson's book. Watson is the author of many books on the paranormal. In his *Science: Good, Bad and Bogus* (1981) Martin Gardner commented on one of Watson's books: "[This book] reaches crowning heights of claptrap. . . . [It] is not fun to read unless you are as gullible as he in believing fifty impossible things before breakfast."

Ferguson has much to say on health care, strongly supporting holistic medicine. On the power of prayer: "In an elegantly designed double-blind experiment, an American cardiologist reported that prayer by others significantly affected recovery." She makes no reference to the doctor's name or the date and place of the experiment. This is not remarkable. In books by occultists, seldom does one find references for their claims or see documentation of them.

Ferguson writes that in 1977 she sent questionnaires to 210 people in different walks of life soliciting their opinions on many esoteric subjects. Here are a few of the results regarding strongly held beliefs: Belief in telepathy, 96 percent; in psychic healing, 94 percent; in precognition, 89 percent; consciousness surviving bodily death, 76 percent. Scientific polls taken in recent years are only about half as discouraging.

One wonders if Marilyn Ferguson, when she wrote this book, could have foreseen the wave of flummery it helped to produce. What does Ferguson herself feel about all this flimflam? "I think that phenomena like channeling and the effect of crystals [are] not the main point of what the New Age is about. . . . The same thing with so-called past-life experiences. They can be extremely helpful to people, and we don't have to know whether they were authentic or not."

This typifies the philosophy of New Agers. Yes, some of the deceptive practices of the modern gurus *are* sometimes psychologically helpful to some individuals. But they totally ignore the harm they can cause. And to state that "we don't have to know whether they were authentic or not" indicates a callous disregard for truth. Ferguson is saying that charlatans who fleece the public with their hypocrisy are doing it for our own good.

The New Age is an offshoot of the counterculture movement of the 1960s. The young people involved at that time are now approaching middle age. They represent the majority of those attending the seminars held by Shirley MacLaine, J. Z. Knight, and other high-profile gurus.

This developing movement has taken on a life of its own, and a jargon of its own. Don't try to argue with a New Ager. They'll retaliate with talk of "higher consciousness," "love energies," and "this is my own reality," leaving you shaking your head in bewilderment.

They are taught to be self-loving and self-dependent. Isn't that strange, when you consider that they go to channelers and pay money to get advice from spirits inhabiting another world; that they spend time visiting psychic advisers and astrologers who become authorities they look up to.

Are these often affluent and productive members of society any different from the poor souls who followed Jim Jones to Guyana?

Earlier, I mentioned the "me" generation. This narcissistic trend is just as alive today as it was in the 1970s and it is one of the foundations of what we call the New Age. Self-respect is a necessary and helpful commodity, but the New Age movement is based more on self-infatuation than on self-respect. And it is developing into a new religion.

The idea being sold is that inside every human being there is a wonderful and talented personality. And this personality will grow and flourish if the individual just looks inward and ignores any consideration for others. Just do whatever you feel like doing. This will help you expand your consciousness and make you more self-aware—whatever that means. This nonsensical idea has sold many books and crowded many seminars for a number of years. And it is being exploited today with some new wrinkles.

Where would the graduates of the "human potential" movement—who are now part of the New Age movement—be today if their parents and doctors and teachers and others who nurtured and serviced them in the 1960s and 1970s followed their philosophy?

Ten or fifteen years ago these New Agers were searching for identity. Many of them are still searching. They claim that they don't know who they are. What they really mean is that they are not satisfied with who they are. But it is sometimes not easy to face that fact. So they turn to those who will give them a fast fix.

But it doesn't work. Those who promise to lead the identity-seekers out of their wilderness are false prophets. That is one of the basic problems of the New Age. There is no fast fix, no instant solution.

This business of "finding yourself" defeats its purpose. It does not make for inner happiness. The concept of "losing yourself" makes more sense. You lose yourself when you are immersed in creative activities, when you are involved in helping others, when you get your mind outside yourself. That is when you come to terms with life and get a feeling of self-worth.

Apart from the tendency of the New Age followers to buy the self-love teachings of the movement's leaders, it is difficult to believe that so many reasonably intelligent people can swallow all the paranormal nonsense that is being fed them.

Shirley MacLaine herself seems a little surprised by it all. In her book *It's All in the Playing* (1987) she writes about her many appearances on television and radio call-in shows, and comments that of the hundreds of people who called in not one criticized her for her remarkable statements about psychic matters. Or, as she puts it, "not one person said, 'This stuff is crazy.'"

Having watched some of these programs, I can verify Shirley's comment. People were phoning in to discuss past-life recall, color therapy in healing, and their UFO experiences. They were continually asking Shirley for advice: what books did she suggest they read, what channelers should they visit, and so on. This did not apply only to the people calling in, the studio audience usually got into the act too—with the same results.

If MacLaine was surprised by all this, I was not. For many years I have appeared with psychics, faith healers, astrologers, palm readers, and mediums on various television and radio programs, and I still do. The usual format is for the psychics to come on first to do their shtick ("readings" for members of the studio audience), and then I am interviewed and asked to state my opinions on their presentations. This naturally precipitates an argument between myself and the other guests on the panel, with members of the studio audience chiming in, and then the phone lines are opened.

Two things usually happen at this point: (1) the people in the studio audience side with the psychic; (2) the people who phone in ignore me completely and want to speak to the psychic. Some of them ask for psychic advice then and there! True, occasionally a caller will sound rational and support my views, but this is relatively rare.

The reaction of Shirley MacLaine's audience does not surprise me in the least. It is reasonable to argue that people who get up early in the morning and rush to a downtown studio to catch a MacLaine show would be supporters of Shirley and her wacky theories, and that the millions who watch or listen to the broadcasts are also in the pro-MacLaine category.

But the frightening thing is that there are so many of

them. And the numbers, as indicated by every poll, are growing. If you have any question in your mind about the growth and establishment of the New Age movement, consider this: A directory called *The National New Age Yellow Pages* is now being published. And where is it being published? In California, not too surprisingly. It is being billed as "A United States Guide to Consciousness-Raising Services, Products, and Organizations." Let your fingers do the walking through these pages and you'll have no trouble finding enough contacts to relieve you of your hard-earned bucks. And to get you caught up in a bizarre world of make-believe.

The Christian church sees the New Age movement as a real threat. Many in the church first saw it as a form of fringe lunacy. Now they seem to be taking it more seriously. The subtle ways in which New Agers are drawn in compares unfavorably with the open commitment to faith required by the church.

To the follower of traditional religious teachings, the New Age promotes idolatry and self-worship, turns God into an impersonal energy source, and rejects sin and moral guilt.

*   *   *

Why, in these relatively sophisticated times, do so many believe in the nonsensical drivel encompassed by the New Age— the paranormal and occult nonsense now distributed so efficiently by modern communication techniques? And, make no mistake, efficient it is. If you own a computer and a little device called a modem, you can now hook into a worldwide network that distributes paranormal misinformation without leaving your chair.

It is not my intention in this book to present a scholarly treatise on the psychology of belief. I'll leave that to others more qualified. But I would like to set down a few of what

I think are the reasons that so many otherwise rational people are hooked on the paranormal and all its ramifications.

I've already mentioned how the New Agers are interested in the "fast fix" in order to "find themselves." We are in an age of instant solutions: instant coffee, instant news, instant cash. We are all being conditioned to hurry up.

Let me digress for a moment. I mentioned computers. New programs are constantly being developed. The people who produce these programs run out of ideas for new software. So they merely make clones of the old programs, but the new ones are more "powerful." Which means, among other things, that they run faster. Which means that you can save time when you use them. Sometimes you can save almost five seconds here and there.

Think of the longer, fuller, and more satisfying life you can have by saving those few precious seconds!

And, if you want another example of our new age of hurry, hurry, sit in your car while waiting for a red stoplight to change at an intersection. When it turns green, hesitate for a fraction of a second before taking off. Then count the number of horns you hear blaring behind you.

Now just turn this around and reflect on a strange experience you have undergone. Let us suppose you had a dream that cousin Clarence, living on the other side of the continent, had a serious accident and was in the hospital. And, by golly, the next day you found it had actually happened. It would make you think.

But the next day your problem is solved—instantly. You pick up a book by Shirley MacLaine, or some other purveyor of the paranormal, and read how precognitive dreams are a dime a dozen, and that, not to worry, we are all "psychic."

If you have been raised in an even slightly superstitious environment you will probably be inclined to accept the instant explanation. Indeed, this might just propel you into becoming a true believer, particularly if you read this "explanation" in several different publications, by several different "authorities."

On the other hand, would you be among the minority who would take the time and the trouble to search for a more rational explanation? If you did, you might possibly remember that Clarence had great fun riding his motorcycle at high speed down busy thoroughfares and that you had often thought he was inviting trouble. One night those thoughts might have coalesced into a dream, and it might have been one of those coincidences when the dream tied up with the event.

If you searched further, you might even find that the dream happened *after* the event, not before. After all, most of these anecdotes are related years after they take place, and our memories do play strange tricks. And you might also consider all the thousands of dreams you had experienced in your lifetime that did not coincide with any actual events.

This happening, this personal so-called psychic experience, is one of the factors that can sometimes trigger psychic beliefs. And the desire for the instant explanation, no matter how irrational, encourages the adoption of those beliefs.

Shirley MacLaine makes a fetish out of claiming that we construct our own reality. Those who support this cop-out are merely saying they cannot cope with the actual reality of everyday living. By adopting this philosophy they are latching on to a belief system that seems to guarantee certainty. But there is no certainty in our daily existence.

The dramatic rise of science in the past hundred years, and of science and technology in the past few decades, has paradoxically driven many people into occult beliefs. Many feel a lack of personal control in their lives, that they are just pawns in a vast, impersonal universe. The mystics and the paranormalists condemn science as just another form of religion. The believers feel that the hodgepodge of mumbo jumbo that these people offer gives them a better sense of control. This, they feel, is the only alternative to the outdated traditional religions and the evils of science.

It is ironic, then, that pushers of the paranormal try to use science to justify many of their occultist claims, just as spiritualist frauds of past centuries used religion to hoodwink the public. Of course, many television evangelists and channelers still do. But science and scientific terminology is now being used by New Agers to excite popular interest in the paranormal.

This is comparatively easy to do, because science itself is making so many discoveries of seemingly miraculous things that miracles are becoming almost commonplace in our daily lives. If we can walk on the moon, or watch pictures of events that are happening on the other side of the world at the same instant, what's the big deal if a man says he can pick up your inner thoughts from ten feet away, or that he can levitate and float in the air, or that he can astrally project himself to Mars and back in the twinkling of an eye?

The answer is that there's just one difference: the matter of proof. It is one thing to make a claim, another to prove it. It is also necessary to have a theory to explain it. And the burden of proof is on the claimant, not on the skeptic who questions the claim. And, to this day, there never has been any strong evidence for any of the claims of psychic phenomena—never.

*   *   *

The general public probably got its first inkling of what the New Age was about when the big Harmonic Convergence caper took place on the weekend of August 16 and 17, 1987. The world press and electronic media had a story they couldn't ignore—and the New Age movement got millions of dollars worth of free publicity worldwide. Never have so many people on our planet been fed so much nonsense in so short a time. It's difficult to pin down the original source of this extraordinary production, but it is interesting to note which individuals benefited most from the media exposure.

José Arguelles and Shirley MacLaine were the two names that popped up most often in the news stories I read and on the television and radio shows I monitored. Arguelles, an art historian by training, from Boulder, Colorado, is claimed to be the founder of the Harmonic Convergence movement. According to a story in the *Wall Street Journal*, Arguelles is "a 'millenialist' by inclination, by divine direction, by the dictates of reincarnation." He claimed that, on a particular weekend, a bright new era for mankind would be ushered in. At that time the earth would begin to slip out of its "time beam" and we mortals would feel disoriented.

Arguelles dredged up the whole thing by studying the ancient Mayan calendars. A "great cycle" was shown to run from 3113 B.C. to A.D. 2012—a "galactic beam" 5,125 years in diameter. At the end of the cycle, claimed Arguelles, the earth would shoot out of the beam and into a "galactic synchronization phase." And twenty-five years before its exit (August 16 and 17, 1987) the occupants of this planet would face the responsibility of keeping Mother Earth on course. Hence the necessity for the Harmonic Convergence—to pool our psychic powers and influence our cosmic destiny.

At this time, he announced, believers would experience repeated déjà vu, and UFOs would be arriving in great numbers. A new beginning could be assured only if enough people gathered at designated sacred spots around the globe. This, he claimed, would be the beginning of a New Age. Toronto's *Globe and Mail* ran a story on August 14, 1987 that recounted many of Arguelles's predictions. Most of these are contained in his book *The Mayan Factor* (1987).

The followers of this event said that it would give birth to an unavoidable transformation that would eventually abolish government, religion, and business as we know them. Instead, we would have a heaven on earth in which people would follow their feelings rather than their intellects and become at one with the universe. This would be a critical time for the emergence of new energy on the planet.

These are typical vacuous New Age observations that make no sense whatsoever. Just try to imagine a world where everyone—from those on the lowest rungs of the social ladder to the politicians and statesmen who guide our national destinies—is guided by his or her emotions.

The Harmonic Convergence idea caught on because, to New Age adherents, it offered instant confirmation of many of their beliefs. It was an exotic blend that was particularly attractive to people dissatisfied with traditional religions, and served up in a brief two-day period.

This mix included prophecies, astrological predictions, and UFOs—with a promise of peace and harmony. The ceremonies held at the various gatherings included chanting, dancing in witches' circles, and other rituals dear to the hearts of the mystically inclined.

Some believers claimed to have planned to attend observances at the sacred sites—the Great Pyramid was one of them—even before hearing about the official Harmonic Convergence. They were called, they say, by an inner compulsion (extrasensory perception?) that told them they must be at those places.

In the *Albuquerque Journal* of July 26, 1987 Julian Spalding, one of the event's organizers, sounded a dire warning for those who would not participate: "These energies are essentially forcing people to separate like oil and water into camps of fear and love." He continued, "So we're going to see an increasing number of people turning to fear and greater denial and resistance, and other people turning to love and greater acceptance and openness."

Jim Berenholtz, another organizer, affirmed Spalding's sentiments: "Those who resist the changes will suffer the consequences. They're going to feel a lot of difficulty and stress, physically through disease, emotionally, psychologically, on all different levels."

Here we have an example of New Age occultist behavior: the threat, the establishment of fear. "Do it our way, or else."

However, those who could not feel it in their hearts to participate needn't be too concerned, because this Harmonic Convergence organizer in Albuquerque was already planning a series of seminars to set them on the right path.

The Harmonic Convergence was touted as an event that would usher in a new age, but of course we know that the New Age began some years ago. You'll recall the "Age of Aquarius" from the 1960s rock musical *Hair*. But we are now into a new age of the New Age, if you get the drift. And who's to say how many more new ages there will be. Sooner or later some of them will have to be discarded and relegated to Old Age. And if this nonsense continues to grow, we'll probably end up with another Stone Age.

Another reason for choosing that particular date for the Harmonic Convergence was that the nine planets were supposed to be gathered on one side of the sun, which signaled that five thousand years of hell had just terminated and that we were now due for five thousand years of heaven. It was truly a time for rejoicing, for concentrating mass energies toward a better world.

The faithful did gather, in large numbers. They assembled at various "power points" around the globe—at Niagara Falls, at Mount Shasta in California, at the Great Pyramid in Egypt, at Stonehenge in England, at Machu Picchu in Peru, at Central Park in New York City, at Mount Fuji in Japan.

José Arguelles had announced that there would have to be a minimum attendance of 144,000 believers in order to "create a field of trust, to ground the new vibrational frequencies coming in at that time."

Whether he achieved his quorum I cannot say. Evidently it was poorly organized, and no one took an accurate worldwide headcount. We can only hope and pray that the minimum numbers were reached; otherwise we will not be saved.

But, seriously, is it not interesting to contemplate how this event was publicized and organized on so wide a scale and was carried out on the scheduled date—all without a hitch? Could there be something, after all, to Marilyn Ferguson's revelation of a worldwide New Age network, as mentioned earlier? Surely we cannot attribute the whole thing to telepathy?

* * *

The quartz crystal has become the symbol of the New Age movement. Once again the New Age occultists have taken something old and transformed it into something new.

For many years the word "crystal" was associated with the occult only by the crystal ball, the time-honored tool of the gypsy fortune-teller.

The practice of staring into this supernatural sphere to get a glimpse of the future originated in ancient times. It was called "scrying," from the Middle English word *descry* meaning "to make out dimly, to succeed in discerning, to perceive something unclear or distant." The original crystal balls were made of polished rock crystal. Today, most of the ones on sale at occult shops are made of glass—some are even plastic.

Much of the scrying done in ancient times by necromancers was performed without a crystal ball. Any shiny or polished surface would do. The ancient Greeks economized by gazing into pools of water or a polished metal mirror. The Egyptians favored a pool of blood—certainly lending a more mystical air than a piece of crystal. Even concentrating on a polished fingernail was acceptable.

Using a crystal ball today is considered out of fashion by state-of-the-art psychics and channelers. It is now basically the property of the back parlor, five-dollars-a-visit fortune-teller who specializes in ripping off the really gullible devotee, who will more than likely be advised to bring a newspaper-wrapped package of money for the diviner to retain for safekeeping.

But for those who still do gaze into a crystal ball's murky interior, certain rules and regulations apply. The ball should be at least the size of a small orange. I suppose if it were smaller, you would have to either squint or gaze with one eye at a time. It should never be handled by anyone other than the owner, lest the magnetisms be mixed and the sensitivity be destroyed.

Should such a calamity befall a crystal ball, it can be remagnetized. This is an exact procedure that must not be varied. One must make passes over it with the right hand for at least five minutes at a time. I'm assuming, of course, that we're referring to a right-handed crystal ball. This procedure gives the ball more power. Passes made with the left hand add to its sensitivity. I am uncertain whether these passes should be made in a back and forth or circular motion, and, if circular, whether clockwise or counterclockwise. I would suggest trying both methods.

There is, of course, nothing supernatural about crystal gazing. It does have an effect on some people, but has nothing to do with any particular properties of the crystal. The action of concentrating on the reflective surface of the ball will cause some people to hallucinate or will help produce a form of mental imagery. This imagery can sometimes be so vivid that the individual believes he or she is seeing an actual scene. It has absolutely nothing to do with prophecy, with seeing into the past, or with clairvoyance. It is simply a product of the subject's imagination. The person who claims to see things in a crystal ball, if he's not faking completely, is likely also to be one who claims to see ghosts.

The transition from the use of the crystal ball to the worship of the quartz crystal by New Agers has no parallel in occult history, in its scope or in its speed. My personal exposure to this crystal revolution has happened just in the past year or two. I can cite two examples of the crystal craze that impressed me.

For a number of years I have attended many of the psychic fairs that have been held in cities and towns across the continent. I have not spent hours at these dispensaries of nonsense just to be masochistic. As a writer and debunker of the paranormal, duty dispatches me to many strange places.

These fairs are getting bigger, but I can't say better. They usually consist of dozens, even hundreds of booths. The booths are occupied by psychics, astrologers, and clairvoyants of every description who give readings to the hungry attendees at anywhere from $25.00 to $100.00 a crack. There are also many booths set up as retail outlets for occult wares—crystals, occult books, aura charts, sandals that diagnose your physical ailments, but strangely enough no fortune cookies.

It has been interesting to observe the changes that have taken place over the years, because these changes reflect those taking place in the New Age movement.

The number of psychics doing tealeaf readings and plotting astrology charts has declined. There has been a steady increase in the use of computers and computer printouts, reflecting our high-tech culture. No longer does the dark-haired lady hold your hand as she reads your palm. Now you just stick out your hand and tear off the paper that rolls out of the printer.

But the most dramatic change that I have seen has been in the proliferation of booths selling crystals. Just two years ago, at one of the psychic fairs I attended, there was exactly one booth dispensing crystals. The rather bored-looking woman tending the display aroused my curiosity, because she was the only vendor without customers. She was just standing there, guarding a skimpy assortment of colorless crystals, looking as if she wished she were somewhere else.

Out of sympathy, I walked over and inquired about her wares. She seemed relieved that at least someone was engaging her in conversation. Having done my good deed for the day, I strolled away to acquire a psychic reading at one of the other booths, where I was told by the resident swami that I was an intuitive believer in almost everything!

A few months ago I attended a later version of that same fair, and for me it was a shocker. There were booths dispensing crystals as far as the eye could see, in a hall about as big as an airplane hangar. They were literally all over the place. The variety of crystals on display—in different shapes, sizes, and colors—was immense. Almost every booth had several customers around it. And they were *buying*! It's crystal clear that the crystal has taken over.

I have been given another view of what has been happening on the crystal scene in my role as guest on television talk-shows. For many years I have participated on these programs, usually as a counterbalance to the other guests. These would usually be an assortment of so-called psychics, faith healers, astrologers, palm readers, pundits, and others of that fraternity. Never once, in all those years, in all those debates, was the subject of crystals mentioned, either by my opponents, by the studio audiences, or by the people phoning in.

During the past year the crystal enthusiasts have been

coming out of the woodwork. Every show I have been on has included at least one guest who has jumped on the crystalline bandwagon.

Connie Church, author of *Crystal Clear* and *Crystal Love*, appeared with me on "The Oprah Winfrey Show" of January 14, 1988. When Oprah called on various members of the audience for their questions and opinions, the crystal people were hopping up from all over. Some expressed learned opinions about crystal energy; others were in the business and made a sales pitch.

So, there's no question: The crystal has definitely grabbed a large slice of the occult market and is here to stay, at least until some new craze develops. And I believe it's fair to say that the exploitation of the quartz crystal by the New Age movement is the first really new paranormal addition to its arsenal of nincompoopery.

It would now be appropriate, I think, to take a look at the quartz crystal and see what claims are being made for its mystical properties—and then to describe its true properties.

Quartz crystals have the unique property of containing an active electrical element that seems to give them life. The occultists, quick to capitalize on any scientific fact that could possibly add to their storehouse of mumbo-jumbo, have thus adopted the crystal as their pet artifact. They speak of its living properties, its healing energies, its ability to amplify sound, thoughts, and whatever. They attribute to it every power their imaginations can dream up.

The bizarre anecdotes about the use of crystals keep multiplying. A former marketing consultant in Philadelphia uses crystals to help her houseplants grow and to get rid of headaches (hers, not the plant's). A Manhattan businessman keeps crystals in his pocket to aid concentration and improve his talents for negotiation. Actress Jill Ireland wrote *Life Wish* (1986), a book about using crystals in her battle with breast cancer. A Texas rancher uses crystals to keep flies away from his cattle. Several chiropractors use crystals as part of their treatments.

In California, a veterinarian hangs crystal pendants around the necks of all her patients. A retired scientist works in a million-dollar laboratory using a special piece of apparatus and an antenna. He claims he can broadcast an energy charge from himself into a crystal, and from there to another person. Some experts claim that crystals can be programmed like a computer by using heavy doses of meditation; a popular program is one that has the crystal maintain your "emotional stability and physical balance." One Denver resident keeps her crystal collection buried outside her house—to ward off intruders.

The owner of the Crystal Galleries (a legitimate gem-dispensing establishment) in Boulder, Colorado, had to move his quartz crystals to the rear, because too many passersby came in and lounged around for hours, absorbing crystal power. When they began to put their heads between two crystals, the management decided that enough was enough.

Although the use of crystals has exploded in the New Age, the occult powers attributed to this common gem can be traced back to ancient times and mythologies. Crystals were used as talismans in the warrior's armor to protect him from his enemies. Ancient kings mounted crystals in their crowns. In the Middle Ages, alchemists and sorcerers constructed long metal tubes and installed crystals at the tips, in order to dispense magical energies. This is alleged to be the precursor of the "magic wand."

Today there are so many different powers attributed to the crystal that their dispensers can't lose. What can this magical stone do for you? Just look at the hype on the back cover of Gari Gold's book *Crystal Energy* (1987), subtitled "Put the Power in the Palm of Your Hand." Explore your own untapped energies by: clearing away negative attitudes; centering personal energies; enhancing communication; promoting healing (from allergies to headaches); opening the heart to love and courage; simplifying decision making; balancing the spirit; focusing the mind; tapping into psychic powers; using chakra and colors. Gari Gold, by the way, is a "gem therapist who has studied vibrational healing."

Gold's book contains a good example of the convoluted logic that New Agers swallow without questioning. After outlining some unsubstantiated facts about the energies emitted by crystals and about their healing powers, the author writes: "If there is any doubt in your mind that a seemingly inanimate object like a rock can actually affect your health, I'd like to ask you at this point to consider the repercussions of being very close to uranium. Uranium is a dangerous radioactive substance that looks like an innocent rock. There are no easy signs to tell you that it is vibrating at a rate that is completely destructive to your physical body. While uranium has been found to have a bad effect on us, quartz and other gemstones usually have a positive effect on us, and can be used in a number of ways to benefit our physical, emotional, and mental selves."

Gold conveniently disregards the fact that the radioactive properties of uranium have been established, but that there is absolutely no evidence whatever that crystals emit curative energies. In fact, unless acted upon physically, they just lie there, emitting nothing. And at no time, even when physically vibrated, do they send out any measurable form of energy beyond the surface of the crystal. More on that later.

The only positive effect that I can see in carrying around a crystal would be as a good luck charm, equivalent to putting a rabbit's foot in your pocket, or hanging a horseshoe over your doorway. If it gives you a sense of security, great. It certainly is more convenient than dragging around your favorite blanket.

As for its healing powers, in some cases it could have the same effect as the laying on of hands. This is the placebo effect, and it would apply only to psychosomatic illnesses or to hysterical symptoms, where, for example, the person has been subjected to some mental trauma that has had a temporary physical effect on the body.

But to claim that crystals can heal organic diseases is to be dishonest, fraudulent, and potentially harmful. When the "crystal healer" has you lie down, places different colored crystals on various parts of your anatomy, and feeds you the baloney about influencing your health through your "chakras," you should know you're in the hands of a charlatan.

Now the argument has been presented to me that I should not brand these people charlatans in such a wholesale fashion, that some of them are just deluded, but mean well. There's a problem here. How does anyone know whether someone is deluded or is consciously motivated to practice deception? I can think of only one way to settle this controversy. Let us just call these people "unconscious charlatans" and let it go at that.

So much for the so-called occult properties of the crystal. What science has to say is a little different, and it is backed up by incontrovertible evidence.

When you walk along a beach you are walking on quartz. You are also walking on the most common mineral on the planet. Quartz is a silicon dioxide, and when the forces of the wind and the waves break it up into tiny pieces we have what we call sand. When sand is melted at very high temperatures and then cooled, we end up with what is called fused quartz. When silicates (compounds containing silicon) are added, and if this is then melted, it will become what we know as glass. If it is cooled very slowly, quartz will crystallize, forming six-sided, or hexagonal, internal structures.

When all this happens in nature, the various impurities captured in the crystals will give them different colors, which then convert the crystals into the recognizable gems: agate, amethyst, aquamarine, tourmaline, and so on. One of the softer and more inferior of the gems is the quartz crystal, which is the one most exploited in the field of the occult.

The only energy known to science that is associated with the quartz crystal is something called the "piezoelectric effect." If you create a physical pressure on one side of the crystal it will distort it, and create an internal electrical imbalance. This will produce a tiny electrical charge on the opposite face of the crystal. On the other hand, if you wire up both sides of the crystal to an electrical circuit with a battery in it, and place an electrical charge on one side, it will cause the crystal to distort.

Taking this one step further, if the crystal is wired into a circuit with a varying electrical current, there will be an ongoing vibration of the crystal in proportion to the change of voltage on it. And as a last step, if the crystal is physically caused to vibrate at varying frequencies, it will produce proportional varying voltages in the electrical circuit.

This is exactly what happens in your standard record player. The needle, or stylus, is connected to a thin sliver of crystal that has a wire connected to each side. The needle vibrates in the record groove according to the frequencies impressed on it. This causes the crystal to vibrate at these frequencies and transmits the varying voltages to your amplifier, which amplifies these voltages enough to move the cone on your loudspeaker, which produces the sound waves in the air, and which, finally, your ears pick up.

Science and technology have found ways to make other practical uses of these properties of the crystal. Hooking one up to an appropriate electronic circuit produces a continuous vibration of the crystal. This vibration, according to the size and shape of the crystal, can be set at a predetermined frequency that is extremely accurate and stable. That's how the quartz crystal is applied to your wrist watch and other technological miracles.

If you have patiently followed this primer on electronics to its conclusion, you can see that the crystal does have special properties, but not the mystical powers attributed to it by paranormalists.

In the meantime, despite the complete lack of scientific evidence that crystals emit some mysterious energies that influence health and happiness, the business of selling them for this purpose has increased dramatically. And the great demand has caused the prices to skyrocket. Occultist entrepreneurs are cashing in on a bonanza.

*   *   *

If I were asked to name one particular reason why the New Age philosophy has spread so rapidly in the 1980s, I would attribute it to book publishers, major and minor.

There has always been a ready market for books on the occult and the pseudosciences, whether they were novels, mystical tracts, so-called true stories (*The Amityville Horror* [1977] and *The Bermuda Triangle* [1974]), or self-help pop psychology involving one's mythical psychic abilities. But now, with a new umbrella term—the "New Age"—to group all these categories together, the whole thing has really taken off.

This has helped the books' sales enormously. Booksellers are now scrapping many of the categories in which they formerly displayed their books and now group everything under "The New Age," which includes books on mysticism, psychic phenomena, UFOs, astrology, channeling, reincarnation, crystal healing, and occult subjects. In addition, many of the books that were previously displayed in scattered sections, such as philosophy, self-help, business and management, women's studies, psychology, and even science, are now added to the New Age roster.

This emphasizes what has been happening in the real world. The tentacles of this movement have spread out to encompass a huge variety of subjects, and to draw in a much wider audience than would be interested only in the occult. The New Age has now become a generic term for those interested in metaphysics, spiritualism, alternative medicine, and a hodgepodge of faddist ideas. And the book publishing and distributing industry is selling it, hard.

Interest in various aspects of the paranormal and the occult has always had its peaks and valleys. For example, astrology has gone through periods of popularity and neglect for thousands of years. The modern flying-saucer flaps have also had their ups and downs. And book publishers in recent years have followed these trends.

Reincarnation became a hot topic back in the 1950s, when Morey Bernstein wrote his best-selling *The Search for Bridey Murphy* (1956). This allegedly true story was about an American woman who was hypnotically regressed to a previous life she had lived in Ireland. The fact that a more rational explanation was found for her "memories" had little effect on the sale of the book. It continued to keep the reincarnation pot boiling.

Now, with Shirley MacLaine's books selling reincarnation once more, the subject is hotter than ever. Note a few recent titles: *Reincarnation: A New Horizon in Science; The Case for Reincarnation; Past Lives, Future Loves; You Were Born Again to be Together; Bridge Across Forever; Born Again and Again; Lifetimes: True Accounts of Reincarnations; Reincarnation and Eternal Love; Life between Life; Your Past Lives: A Reincarnation Handbook; Past-Life Regression; Experiencing Reincarnation; Reincarnation for the Christian.*

One reincarnation book stands out, in my opinion, because of its intriguing content. It's called *The Search for Omm Sety: Reincarnation and Eternal Love.* It's the story of an Englishwoman who, through astral projection, continues an affair with an Egyptian pharaoh begun three thousand years ago. Shirley MacLaine's story of reuniting, as a lover, with a former past-life acquaintance (in her book *Out On a Limb* [1983]) is rather pallid compared to this one.

A survey of the New Age books now dominating the market places the subjects of crystals and channeling on top of the heap, along with reincarnation. Just to mention a few of the books on crystals: *Crystal Energy; Crystal Clear; The Crystal Oracle; Crystal Tree; Crystal Power; The Crystal Handbook; The Crystal Sourcebook; Clearing Crystal Consciousness; The Crystal Healing Book; Healing with Crystals and Gemstones; Healing with Crystal and Color Therapy; Crystal Enlightenment; Crystal Love; Crystal Woman; Stone Power; The Crystal Book; The Cosmic Crystal Spiral.* Again, these are just a few of the titles available on the New Age bookshelves. Several of these books have stones packaged with them—a good sales gimmick. *The Crystal Oracle* includes several colored stones along with a velour mat. The book itself contains a guide on how to use the stones and the mat to do your own readings.

These books are no longer sold only in bookshops. They are now being peddled in gem stores opening in major cities all over the continent.

In 1987 the top-selling New Age books included those on UFOs, with the alleged abductions grabbing the spotlight. *Communion* (1987), Whitley Strieber's imaginative tale of his own experiences at the hands of the little people from outer space, hit the *New York Times* bestseller list and stayed there for weeks.

Budd Hopkins wrote *Intruders* (1987), which detailed the

abductions of dozens of hapless individuals who related their experiences to him under hypnosis. He is still cashing in on the book by towing some of these people along with him to relate their fantasies on television talk shows. I've labeled this phenomenon *Abductio ad Absurdum*.

The UFO craze seemed to have subsided in recent years. I didn't know whether to attribute it to a return to sanity or to the media and the publishers merely tiring of it all. Then the New Age appetite for anything titillating took over. Writing a book on UFO sightings was too mild. Wholescale abductions would be the logical way to go. And these books' sales really took off.

At this writing, even interest in UFO abductions is beginning to taper off. Somebody is going to have to come up with a new scheme. How about us humans abducting some of the little extraterrestrials? An enterprising author can call this sure-fire best-seller "The Grabbing of the Green Men: A True Story." I wish I could take credit for this idea, but I must give the honor to whom it is due. Fred D. Baldwin, a writer from Carlisle, Pennsylvania, wrote an article for *Omni* magazine in which he claimed that these abductions have already happened, and are repeated daily. This article is obviously written in a satirical manner, and by itself is quite humorous.

But no publisher would be interested in a book of this kind. It would have to be labeled "a true story," no matter how incredible the contents. Then it can't miss.

Actually, Baldwin credits the events he outlines to one Dr. Perry Noya (pronounce that quickly), the "author" of *Aliens in Our Attics*. He writes, "People who conceal aliens in their homes are reluctant to own up to it, either because they are worried about attracting the attention of the Immigration and Naturalization Service, or they are afraid their property values will plummet."

Baldwin tells of his interview with Noya. When asked what kind of people would hold an innocent tourist from another solar system "against his or her will," Noya answered, "Lonely people. A few are kids, but most seem to be senior citizens. Most people aren't necessarily monsters, but some definitely exploit aliens. For example, my files document cases of freon-exhaling visitors from Venus kept in commercial garages by heating contractors and forced to recharge old air-conditioning units."

Noya claims that federal agencies are using extraterrestrial illegals in various government departments, and they're messing things up. But you just can't fire them. It's impossible to fire someone in a government job, he says, even if he's from another planet.

One of the most shocking things about this story is that some of these little people have died in captivity. And it was discovered that the earth's gravitational field and atmosphere caused their bodies to shrink dramatically into a rubbery substance. Frequently the corpses have been mistaken for the tiny figures one finds as prizes in boxes of cereal. "You'd be surprised how many dead aliens I have found mixed in with a kid's Froot Frosties," said Noya, sadly shaking his head.

He claimed to have discovered a tiny brontosaur and other prehistoric creatures in his cereal. This got him to thinking, and now he is writing a second book, entitled *The Tyrannosaurus at Your Breakfast Table*. Writes Baldwin, "It will offer his theory of what really happened to the dinosaurs."

Another category of books currently sweeping the market are those on channeling, the very questionable practice of speaking to spirits of the dead. These titles are not as numerous as the aforementioned, but they rank high in popularity. Most of them include one of two approaches: a description of what channeling is about, or six easy lessons on how you, too, can be a channeler.

Some of the catchy titles? *Channeling: Speculations on Receiving Information from Paranormal Sources; How to be a Channel; Opening to Channel: How to Connect with Your Guide;* and *We Don't Die: George Anderson's Conversations with the Other Side.* There are many others.

Apart from these current leaders in the field, the old regulars on mysticism, the paranormal, and self-help fads are still rolling along. There is no shortage of choice in such titles as *Creative Visualization: The I Ching on Business and Decision Making; Astral Projection; How to Increase Awareness of Your Inner Guide; Astrology and Your Past Lives; Healing Magnets; Inventing the Future: Advances in Imagery That Can Change Your Life; The Psychic Power of Animals; Holistic Massage; How to Learn from a Course in Miracles; Preparing for the Fifth Dimension;* and *Scentual Touch: A Personal Guide to Aromatherapy.*

And let's not overlook the role that sex plays in the paranormal and the mystical. Publishers know that the word *sex* on a bookcover increases its sale. Some books combining sex with New Age thought are: *Sexual Secrets; The Alchemy of Ecstasy; Sexual Intimacy; Tales of the Sexy Snake;* and *Love, Sex, and Astrology.*

One book that has attracted many readers is *The Book of Runes* (1983), now in a second edition called *The New Book of Runes* (1987). Runes were symbols inscribed on stones and were used by the ancient Vikings, so the story goes, as a form of divination. Anthropologist Ralph Blum, who wrote the book, had a great idea. He had little stones manufactured and inscribed and packaged them with the book. It became a popular parlor game. But, like the Ouija board, it has occult connotations and tremendous appeal to New Agers.

Blum claims that the book, and the use of the runes, connects people with their intuitive process. It is, he says, "a Jungian tool for accessing data from the unconscious."

The book sold 300,000 copies in its first printing, and the second edition is well on its way to that figure.

I would make a suggestion to those who wish to save on the price of the book. When you're in the kitchen preparing that delicious chicken dinner, remove the entrails from the bird, spread them out on a table, and interpret their position. You'll get the same results as you will from the runes—maybe better.

I should point out that I'm not trying to provide an educational reading list by bringing these titles to the reader's attention. But it is instructive to read one or two of these books to see how preposterous they can be—and then to ponder that millions of people do buy them and take them quite seriously.

In addition to the glut of New Age books on the market, a new development is New Age audio cassettes. Books on tape were first introduced as readings of the classics and best-selling novels, sometimes read by the author. New Age publishers were quick to spot the potential. They wasted no time in recording a slew of audio cassettes from the nonsense already in print. Then a new factor was introduced: subliminal and hypnotic tapes.

Now, in the comfort of your living room, you can hypnotize yourself subliminally, and astrally project all over the universe. Just be sure to read the intructions before you begin so you won't have a problem returning to your living room. You wouldn't want to end up like that fellow who found himself in the string section of the Cleveland Symphony Orchestra playing "Three Blind Mice."

Or, you can buy a cassette that subliminally teaches you to read auras. Just think of the attention you can attract by telling your friends the color of the sparks shooting out of their ears.

Or, you can learn, subliminally, to take off weight or

quit smoking.

When you play these tapes you're supposed to get into a dreamy mood and listen to the music. There is supposed to be a voice in the background, giving instructions on the particular subject you have chosen. You can't actually hear the voice, but you are supposed to be perceiving it at a subconscious level. In this "subliminal" manner the message is supposed to make a deeper impression.

It is interesting that skeptics who have investigated some of these tapes claim that there is actually nothing on them except the music. But that should make no difference to the true believer, who will probably astrally project anyway.

*   *   *

One of the stranger spinoffs of the New Age movement has been the adoption of many of its tenets by the business world. There have always been a few executives who consulted their astrologers before making important business decisions. But today many of the questionable New Age practices have been adopted and installed by companies as part of their operations.

They hire motivational gurus to hold seminars to change the way their employees think. These gurus are called "consultants." According to an article in the May 4, 1987 issue of *Newsweek,* companies like General Foods, Polaroid, the Ford Motor Company, Procter and Gamble, RCA, Boeing, General Mills, and many others are spending billions on these programs. The old human-potential movement has invaded the boardroom and gained respectability.

In the 1970s, Werner Erhard founded a personal-development program that spread like wildfire. It was known as *est*. When it began to go downhill in the early 1980s, Erhard founded a business designed to do for companies what *est* was supposed to have done for individuals—Transformational

Technologies. The company has been franchised throughout the United States and some major corporations are its clients. The February 9, 1987 issue of *U.S. News and World Report* indicated that critics of these seminars claim that they have caused psychotic breakdowns and even suicides. There have been several lawsuits.

Many employees have complained that these programs use mind-control techniques. The programs are dangerous, they say, because they seek to induce a trancelike state that is intended to clear the mind so that new thoughts and ideas can be implanted to modify a person's behavior. This is reminiscent of the brainwashing techniques used on prisoners of war. Others say that they promote values alien to one's religious beliefs.

In 1987 the California Public Utilities Commission received complaints from employees of Pacific Bell, the state's largest utility, who claimed they had been required to attend seminars based largely on the teachings of George Gurdjieff, the late Russian mystic. Gurdjieff, who died in 1949, launched his system of psychophysical culture in Russia in 1912. It employed various techniques to "break habits of thought and emotion, and awaken a higher consciousness." He devised group exercises involving breathing techniques, music and dance. He built a strong following in the United States when he visited in 1924. His published writings have long been a staple on the shelves of occult bookshops. *Time* magazine described Gurdjieff as a "remarkable blend of P. T. Barnum, Rasputin, Freud, Groucho Marx, and everybody's grandfather." It is difficult to accept that a giant state utility company would adopt and purvey his teachings. Many believe that the trend to corporate use of these unorthodox training techniques are designed to homogenize the thinking of their employees. Some of the programs use hypnosis or meditation along with such techniques.

This trend toward adopting New Age methods in employee-training programs has not been limited to corporations. The U.S. Army has also gotten into the act. The *Seattle Times* of January 21, 1987 reports that after the Vietnam war, the Army was ready to try almost anything to improve its image. It set up several centers to explore the idea of combining mindpower with firepower. A think tank was established in the Pentagon to evaluate the paranormal. It consulted people who were proponents of extrasensory perception. It even took the time to evaluate a proposed helmet designed to unite the left and right sides of the brain (to ostensibly combine logical and intuitive thinking in one fell swoop). It might have been more useful to invent a helmet to enable the members of the think tank to think.

A January 21, 1987 article in the *Seattle Times* quotes a Lt. Col. Jim Channon: "When I was in combat, I could sense the presence of other people 400 to 500 meters away without seeing them. That's ESP." Channon invented a fictional unit called the "First Earth Battalion." It would try to stop battles instead of fighting them, or plant trees instead of land mines. He suggested the use of "Warrior Monks" equipped with divining rods and bearing flowers, proposing that they parachute in between two contending armies, unarmed, to deter fighting.

According to the same article, Channon invited 80 army officers to a meeting at Fort Knox, Kentucky. He asked them to remove their shoes. They were taken into a darkened room and seated around a candle burning in the center of the room. They were then asked to suspend their thinking and to intone "e" as a mantra—a ritual sound. Channon then proceeded to describe a day in the life of a soldier in the First Earth Battalion. This mythical battalion later became the label of an actual network of 300 soldiers who served as an Army think tank.

On July 17, 1985, a syndicated article by columnist Jack Anderson gave the shakes to a lot of New Age adherents. The Soviets, he claimed, were outspending the United States by 70 to 1 in occult research. He also revealed that the Pentagon had once considered the development of an "anti-missile time-warp machine" that would blast incoming missiles into a prehistoric era. The Pentagon psychic warriors, wrote Anderson, had been working with annual budgets as high as $6 million.

Anderson said that the CIA had been carefully monitoring Soviet psychic research for years, and estimated that they had been spending hundreds of millions of dollars a year in this field. Hence the "psychic-gap."

Did U.S. intelligence take all this seriously? Well, the Defense Intelligence Agency, according to Anderson, said that the Soviets might one day be able to learn the contents of secret U.S. documents by psychic techniques, make U.S. weapons malfunction by negative thinking, and even brainwash or disable American leaders by willpower.

Ronald McRae, in his book, *Mind Wars* (1984), enlarges on this theme. The book is packed with incredible New Age stories on the psychic activities of the U.S. military. He tells of a Navy commander who visits a Washington, D.C. psychic regularly, and pays her $400 on each visit for a reading. But there's nothing personal about it—it's all in the line of duty. The money comes from the Office of Navy Intelligence, and it's in exchange for photographs and charts of the estimated travel routes of Soviet submarines along the Eastern coast of the United States—all obtained through psychic means.

According to McRae, a former Army intelligence analyst named Thomas Bearden claimed that the army had developed something really sensational, a "hyperspatial nuclear howitzer," a psychic weapon that "could denude the strategic capability of the free world with a single shot by transmitting a single nuclear explosion instantaneously to a limitless number of sites anywhere in the universe."

Again, according to McRae, Congressman Charlie Rose, a seven-term Democrat from North Carolina, called the concept "really something." McRae quotes Rose: "I've seen some incredible examples of remote viewing [the ability to see a distant place telepathically]. I think we ought to pay close attention to developments in this field and especially what the Soviets are doing. If they develop a capacity to have people mentally view secret centers within this country, we could reach the point where we didn't have any secrets."

McRae wrote: "Rose thinks skeptics in the Pentagon and CIA are hindering research in remote viewing, and he wonders openly about their motives. 'We may have to investigate them,' he warns."

If the reader thinks this is a thing of the distant past, consider this: When Uri Geller made his latest tour of the United States in late 1987 promoting his most recent book *The Geller Effect* (1986), he was invited to a Washington, D.C. briefing for a group that was said to include two congressmen and several Capitol Hill and Pentagon aides.

Senate Foreign Relations Committee Chairman Claiborne Pell initiated the invitation and has been quoted as being "stimulated" by Geller's ideas. House Foreign Affairs Committee Chairman Dante Fascell, according to his secretary, rushed out to get a book about Geller.

Just remember this: When you hear of police officers and airline pilots, and presidents of the United States, claiming to have spotted flying saucers and of high public officials and military officers supporting claims of the paranormal, just think of the high degree of gullibility exhibited by ordinary people, as revealed by polls taken over the years. And remember our elected officials and our public servants are ordinary people too.

                    *   *   *

It is ironic that, when many in the Eastern world are swinging away from belief in reincarnation, thousands in the West are latching on to it. And there's little doubt that Shirley MacLaine's constant promotion of her belief in past lives has had an effect on New Agers.

Reincarnation is the belief that the soul travels to another plane upon the death of the body, from where it later returns to take its place in another body at birth. In other words, there is no such thing as a new soul—just a retread.

It is not my intention to present a treatise on reincarnation. I would refer the reader to an excellent discussion of the subject by Paul Edwards in a four-part article beginning in the Fall 1986 issue of *Free Inquiry,* a quarterly magazine, published in Buffalo, New York. But a discussion of New Age trends would not be complete without reference to reincarnation and regressive hypnosis. These, along with channeling and crystal healing, are among the current fads that take top billing.

Reincarnation, of course, has always been a part of Buddhism, Hinduism, and several other Eastern religions. There is a vast amount of literature on the subject. The belief in Karma is included in some of these religions though not all of them. A person's karma is believed to be made up of his actions, good and bad; and his existence in a future lifetime will reap the rewards, or the punishments, of his actions in the previous life.

From a religious or moral viewpoint there is something to be said for this concept. Of course, like all religious beliefs, there is no evidence for these hypotheses—they are based on faith.

But New Agers go a lot further. They can tell you the approximate dates of their past lives, who they were, how they died, and anything else their imaginations can dredge up. And they accept past-life regressive hypnosis as a proved fact, which it is not.

The subject of hypnosis itself is a controversial one. You will find few psychologists who agree as to what the phenomenon really is. But many do agree that a subject undergoing hypnosis is not really unconscious, and that the individual's imagination and fantasizing can come into play and can be manipulated by the hypnotist—just as an accomplished lawyer can lead a witness.

In the highly suggestible state that a person enters under hypnosis, and under the direction of the hypnotist, the subject's "memories" have been shown to be no more accurate than if he were awake; and the more imaginative the subject, the more colorful the details. There is nothing mystical about this procedure.

If a person proposes to undergo hypnosis to dig up a past life, he or she is likely to be a strong believer, and is even more likely to dream up various scenarios that support the premise. Nor is there strong evidence as yet that regressive hypnosis to a younger age in *this* lifetime is valid.

An article in *Omni,* the science-oriented magazine, features an interview with Dr. Ian Stevenson of the University of Virginia. Stevenson, a Canadian-born psychiatrist, is without a doubt the leading guru of Western belief in past lives. He has spent years in researching reincarnation and has published a multitude of papers and books on the subject. Even Shirley MacLaine recognizes him as an authority.

The interview in *Omni* is a rarity. Stevenson invariably refuses to grant media interviews. The reason? He claims to have been tricked by the press and badly "misrepresented." When I called his office some time ago, his secretary told me that I could mail in any questions I had.

Stevenson seems to take the same direction as do many

parapsychologists. He mixes an apparent belief in the paranormal with a desire to approach his subject in a scientific manner. This produces a smorgasbord of apparent facts.

One has to question his scientific objectivity when he admits to still being impressed by the Bridey Murphy case. The "facts" of this case are presented in Morey Bernstein's book *The Search for Bridey Murphy*. This was a sensational case in 1952 when a Colorado housewife named Virginia Tighe, under hypnosis, claimed to have lived another life in Ireland as Bridey Murphy in 1806. This case spawned a book, long-playing records, syndicated newspaper articles and magazine pieces, the sale of movie rights, and worldwide attention. It kicked off a reincarnation craze that swept Western society. The interest eventually waned, until it was again revived by the New Age movement.

The entire Bridey Murphy episode was eventually shown to have a rational explanation. Investigation revealed that a real Bridey Murphy lived across the street from Mrs. Tighe in Chicago when she, Virginia, was a little girl. And the Irish Bridey used to relate anecdotes to the young, impressionable Virginia, telling her detailed stories of events in Ireland at the beginning of the nineteenth century. Under hypnosis, Mrs. Tighe recalled many of these details, and, with the usual type of fantasizing, she projected herself back into that period.

This is a not uncommon type of reaction under hypnosis. The interesting thing is that, after all these years, Dr. Stevenson is still impressed with the original tale.

Stevenson claims that the strongest evidence for reincarnation is the appearance of birthmarks on people who claim to have suffered violent attacks in a previous life. These marks, according to him, are actual scars that have rematerialized in this life. Even if one buys the concept of a spirit being revived, Stevenson has never explained the possibility of the revival of body tissue that has decayed after death.

Stevenson has traveled extensively in India and other Eastern countries, where he has gathered numerous anecdotal accounts, mostly from children, of past life existences. He has written a book entitled *Twenty Cases Suggestive of Reincarnation* (1974) which details his findings. They tell of experiences many years back, in other villages and locations, experiences that Stevenson claims these kids could not have possibly known about unless they had lived in those places in those times.

British author Ian Wilson has investigated many of the cases cited by Stevenson and has raised some interesting points in his book *Mind Out of Time?* (1981). For instance, since written records are rare in these countries, most of the information Stevenson obtained was strictly oral—and even that was shaky, having been obtained by interpreters.

Also, states Wilson, most of the children questioned came from poor families and many of them claimed they had been rich in past lives and asked for portions of the property belonging to their former families.

Stevenson admits that some of the claims could have been fraudulent and that some of the information could have been obtained through natural means. But then, he asks, how about some of the cases where he could find no possible avenues of communication?

Which brings up two points. First, why even publish cases that could have been fraudulent? And, second, this type of rationalization fits in neatly with the thinking of most paranormal supporters: the UFOlogist who says, "Yes, most UFO sightings have been explained, but how about the few that have not been?" Or the believer who says, "True, most psychics are charlatans, but how about those who have never been caught in trickery?"

The burden of proof is on the claimant. And, strangely,

Dr. Stevenson does admit that there is really no proof for reincarnation. But, he says, "As the body of evidence accumulates, it's more likely that more and more people will see its relevance."

Here again he demonstrates a common fallacy of parapsychological thinking: that the greater the quantity of insignificant evidence, the stronger the argument becomes. But the quantity is of no relevance if the *quality* of the evidence is suspect. It will take mighty strong evidence indeed to prove the case for reincarnation.

*   *   *

Another New Age development in the field of the paranormal is the use of psychics in the justice system, and in the field of criminal investigation. These soothsayers have found their way into the legal systems of Europe, Canada, and the United States.

The use of psychics in the courtroom is a new development, but the so-called "psychic detective" has been around for a while. He or she is the one who is brought in by the authorities to find a missing person when the usual police methods have failed. In this New Age the police seem to be more prone to ask for "psychic" assistance than in other years, when the clairvoyant usually volunteered his services. Indeed, some police departments now have psychics listed and call them in even before they have exhausted their standard procedures.

Interestingly, whenever I—or any other skeptical investigators—have taken the trouble to follow up claims that psychics have solved cases for the police, I have come up with a big zero. They have done nothing of the sort.

Take the case, for example, of the psychic Earl Curley, with whom I debated on the "Brian Gazzard Show" (CFCF-

TV, Montreal) in May of 1986. He claimed to have sent information to the FBI that helped nab Wayne Williams, who was convicted of the Atlanta murders of several young children. After the conclusion of the program I called the FBI in Washington, who promptly informed me that yes, this man had volunteered information, but no, it had been of absolutely no help in identifying the suspect.

Then there was Dorothy Allison of Nutley, New Jersey, who also took part in the Atlanta case, but with much more publicity. She got high-voltage media coverage because of super management. When she alighted from the jetliner in Atlanta with reporters swarming around her, you would have thought the president of the United States had just arrived.

After Allison had descended the stairs from the plane she announced into the waiting microphones that she would have the whole matter cleared up in a few days. When she returned to Nutley a few days later, case unsolved, the press didn't bother to announce her failure. It was a nonstory. To this day I meet people who are under the impression that Dorothy Allison helped solve the Atlanta murder case.

Peter Hurkos, the Dutch clairvoyant who saw the psychic light when he fell from a ladder onto his head, also made a reputation for himself as a psychic detective. Hurkos used psychometry as his gimmick. Just hand him an article associated with the missing person and he would find the party, he said. Hurkos the human bloodhound.

He claimed to have helped the police find the infamous Boston Strangler. He thought he had, but it was the wrong man. He also claimed to have drawn a map for British authorities in the highly publicized case of the theft of the Stone of Scone from Westminster Abbey in 1950. The map, said Hurkos, indicated where the Stone would be found. The police later found it, but in a different location. Hurkos took credit for that one too.

In my book *ExtraSensory Deception* (1987), I opened a short piece about Hurkos with: "I wonder what has happened to Peter Hurkos. The celebrated clairvoyant seems to have completely disappeared from the news."

Well, I got my answer a few months ago. Hurkos had been resurrected for the New Age. An older, wearier-looking Peter Hurkos appeared on the "Geraldo" ABC-TV network program as part of a panel pushing the paranormal—an activity to which TV networks are rather prone. On this particular program Hurkos had a stack of items belonging to members of the audience piled in front of him. He was then asked to go into his bloodhound routine.

He picked up a woman's shoe and asked for its owner. This immediately aroused my skeptical instincts. If the man is clairvoyant, why can he not point out the owner, rather than ask her to identify herself. However, in the interest of fair play I decided to overlook this faux pas.

A young woman in the audience stood up. Hurkos gave several personal facts about her. Wrong. Then he got a "hit." "Go to a dentist. You have a toothache." The woman was stunned. "That's right, I do," she replied.

How could Hurkos possibly have known this unless he really was psychic? Here's a hint: A woman sitting next to the subject stood up and said, "It's true. My friend told me she had a toothache." A well-known maneuver by mentalist-magicians is to have an assistant pick up tidbits of conversation from the studio audience before the program airs. This is just one of many methods of securing information. Hurkos's wife, billed as his assistant, sat beside him during the program.

Hurkos was then handed a sealed envelope containing a drawing made by a member of the audience. He handled it for a moment, then announced that it contained the drawing of a house. Wrong. It was a sketch of a pair of lips. Not even close.

But, to me, missing the drawing was not the point. What followed was more revealing. The woman who had submitted the envelope said that, yes, she had originally sketched a house, but then had changed her mind and removed it.

For the uninitiated, one of the standard methods for "psychically" knowing the contents of a sealed envelope is to have someone secretly observe the drawing being made. It's one of Uri Geller's pet deceptions.

Peter Hurkos is no longer with us. The June 2, 1988 issue of the *Los Angeles Times* announced his sudden death due to heart failure. He leaves behind a long trail of controversy.

Another personality on this "Geraldo" program was Dr. Andrija Puharich, introduced as the father of the New Age movement. Puharich is the man who discovered Peter Hurkos and Uri Geller and promoted them in the United States. On this program he made the startling announcement that Peter Hurkos was the chief psychic adviser to the U.S. Navy, and had been for twenty-five years.

Puharich himself has a most interesting background. He is a medical doctor who has patented fifty designs for hearing aids. He is a leading parapsychologist. He wrote a book about Uri Geller entitled *Uri: A Journal of the Mystery of Uri Geller* (1974) in which he stated that Geller gets his revelations from a spacecraft named Spectra that has been stationed over the earth for eight hundred years. Spectra is controlled from a planet named Hoova, according to Puharich. He also touted the infamous Brazilian psychic surgeon, Arigo, known as the "Surgeon of the Rusty Knife."

Puharich may be considered the father of the New Age movement. And Hurkos was resurrected briefly as one of its stars. Shirley MacLaine is one of its leading gurus. With this cast of characters it would seem to be a movement worth watching.

The use of psychics in the justice system in the United States has been proliferating. Psychics are being used in courtrooms to assist in selecting juries. They are even being used as expert witnesses.

There is one lawyer I'm aware of who takes this concept a little further: He himself claims psychic powers. Hugh Silverstein of Rochester, New York, advertises himself as a parapsychologist and claims to use his psychic powers in the courtroom. He asserts that he has the upper hand over opposing lawyers when conducting cross-examination. After all, he knows what the hapless witness is thinking.

Mr. Silverstein, when he's not occupied reading minds in the courtroom, is a regular on the psychic fair circuit, where he dispenses pearls of paranormal wisdom for a fee. I met him at a fair in Toronto a couple of years ago and sat down opposite him for a reading. He told me I was an ardent believer, and always relied on my intuition. I wonder about his winning record in the courtroom.

I also sometimes wonder about the so-called psychics who advertise themselves as *parapsychologists* instead. It does sound more scientific, but are they aware that a parapsychologist is one who studies what some believe to be psychic phenomena, and that a parapsychologist does not claim to have psychic powers. Surely they must understand the lingo of their own trade.

With these paranormal developments in the courtroom, and with the increasing use of clairvoyants by police departments, one begins to wonder where all this will end.

The July 1987 issue of *Omni* carried an essay by the Honorable Howard E. Goldfluss, a justice of the Supreme Court of the State of New York, who informs us that some trial lawyers now have psychics sitting at counsel tables to aid them in the jury selection process. Psychologists have long been used in this process, but the addition of "psychics" adds a new dimension.

Judge Goldfluss lends validity to this practice by citing the case of a defense lawyer in North Carolina whose client was acquitted; the lawyer gives credit to his "psychic" assistant for picking the right jury to influence the verdict.

Goldfluss gives other examples of psychic successes "that even the most jaded and skeptical would find difficult, if not impossible, to ignore."

He is most impressed by Greta Alexander of Delavan, Illinois, who claims she got her psychic powers after being struck by lightning. She evidently has acquired quite a reputation by helping police departments find missing bodies and victims of foul play. The judge mentions a couple of specific cases.

Long on the trail of evidence that would establish the validity of psychic detectives, I phoned Judge Goldfluss in New York to find out where the details of these cases were recorded. Had the judge seen documentation of the exact information supplied by the psychic? Well, no. "But they're in the records of the Delavan police department. [I saw them] quoted in an article I picked up. . . . Contact the Delavan police," said the judge.

The Delavan (population 2,000) police chief was friendly and cooperative. "We have no information, but why don't you call the sheriff of Tazewell County, he should have some." The sheriff was not available, and still has not returned my call.

This has been the scenario for every attempted investigation by this humble skeptic for the past several years. Either the claimed prediction is hazy or the trail fades out.

What is intriguing about the article by Judge Goldfluss is not that psychics are used in courtrooms or that they claim to be of practical assistance to police departments, but that a justice of New York's Supreme Court takes these claims seriously and lends authenticity to them. Does he really believe in psychic powers? Well, regarding Greta Alexander's claimed finding of a homicide victim, "Either she [Greta] committed the murder herself or she had psychic powers," the judge said.

A final question got the answer that perhaps says it all: "Judge Goldfluss, are you aware of any psychic who has been scientifically tested and proved authentic?"

The answer: "No."

The judge, by the way, wrote an earlier article for *Omni,* which appeared the previous month, in which he strongly supported the case for flying saucers. Having been trained in the law, he wrote, there was only one thing that could convince him, and that was good evidence. And he was quite satisfied that the evidence had finally been established. What had convinced him were eyewitness reports from police officers, a couple of scientists, three pilots, and a couple of politicians.

To quote Judge Goldfluss, "We have now heard the other side of the case. We had been led to believe that only charlatans, drunks, fools, or psychopaths observed the phenomenon. We now know that many of those witnesses were responsible, credible, and respected people, most of whom were technologically trained. We now have reason to consider the subject of UFOs in light of strong evidence heretofore suppressed."

The judge is obviously unaware of how many solid citizens in all the categories he mentions have been shown to be inaccurate in their observations of what they thought were alien crafts. If he had read any of Philip J. Klass's books, such as *UFO-Abductions: A Dangerous Game* (1988) and *UFOs: The Public Deceived* (1983), in which some of the most renowned UFO sightings were shown to have prosaic explanations, his certainties might have been shattered.

When I asked him what he thought of the then recent Alaska sighting by an experienced airline pilot, the judge admitted he was unaware of the investigation, and of the explanation—the pilot had observed the planet Jupiter. Surely he knows enough not to make a judgment until all the available facts are in.

Judge Goldfluss, I rest my case.

* * *

Of all the potential harmful effects that can be laid on the doorstep of the New Age movement, I would say that the current promotion of alternative medical practices is the most damaging.

I am referring here to a great variety of practices: holistic medicine; chiropractic; naturopathy; homeopathy; acupuncture; hypnotherapy; health food fads; rolfing; reflexology; herbal medications; biofeedback; chelation therapy; iridology; therapeutic touch; vitamin megadoses; visualization therapy for cancer; crystal therapy; color therapy; body aura cures; and many others.

These various therapies all contain pseudoscientific jargon in their promotional material that sounds impressive to the uninformed public. Which is not to say that some of them don't prove to be helpful, or partially helpful, in *some* cases. But the dangers of relying on these questionable treatments are numerous, as compared to the proved and regulated practices of traditional medicine.

For an in-depth look at alternative medicine I would strongly recommend *Examining Holistic Medicine,* edited by Stalker and Glymour, and also the Fall 1987 *Skeptical Inquirer,* the journal of the Committee for the Scientific Investigation of Claims of the Paranormal. In that issue, there are four excellent articles on questionable therapies, by William

Jarvis, Stephen Barrett, Lewis Jones, and U.S. Congressman Claude Pepper.

Dr. Jarvis, president of the National Council Against Health Fraud, is in a position to know whereof he speaks. In his article he takes a skeptical view of the practice of chiropractic. Judging from the bitter reaction I received from various chiropractic sources after my criticisms in *Extra-Sensory Deception*, I would assume that Dr. Jarvis is receiving his share.

It is impossible to cover the entire field of chiropractic in a limited space, but I believe it is accurate to state that the basic principles upon which the practice is based are not scientifically valid. Chiropractors themselves do not all agree on the proper methodology. They have split into different factions, recommending different kinds of treatment. This does not help to inspire confidence in their profession.

Some chiropractors do help some patients. In cases where merely good manual manipulation is required to treat a fairly simple physical dislocation, the job is done. In other cases, where the problem is psychosomatic and the patient would benefit from the placebo effect of the "laying on of hands," again chiropractic will sometimes help.

But these benefits fall far short of the harm done to many people with serious illnesses who visit chiropractors and really require the services of a physician or surgeon. There have been many reports of spinal cord and other damage due to incorrect chiropractic manipulation.

Of course there are many supporters of chiropractic who will point out that the medical profession has its share of errors and omissions. Unfortunately, this is true. But the built-in system of checks and balances, of supervision and regulation, in the medical field has not been matched by the chiropractors. Neither has the quality of training or the requirements for practice.

Dr. Barrett, writing on homeopathy, points out that it dates back to the late eighteenth century, when a German physician, Dr. Samuel Hahnemann, devised its basic principles. Hahnemann administered herbs, minerals, and other substances to healthy people, and observed the symptoms they produced. Small amounts of these substances were then used to treat patients with similar symptoms. He concluded that these drugs should be administered in as small a dose as possible and that the body would do the rest. Many still practice homeopathy using these principles, although modern pharmacologists believe just the opposite: that the more pronounced the illness, the stronger the dose required.

The January 1987 issue of *Consumer Reports* stated, "Unless the laws of chemistry have gone awry, most homeopathic remedies are too diluted to have any physiological effect. . . . CU's medical consultants believe that any system of medicine embracing the use of such remedies involves a potential danger to patients whether the prescribers are MDs, other licensed practitioners, or outright quacks."

The average alternative therapeutic specialist today spends more time with the patient than do most qualified physicians, thus inspiring confidence and drawing more adherents. British writer Lewis Jones writes of the days when the family physician used to indulge in lengthy chats with the patient and reminds us that this was simply because there was little else he could offer in many cases. With the diagnostic aids available today, the doctor is more likely to get to the crux of the matter in short order and prescribe the proper treatment without the necessity of hand-holding.

Of course, in cases where modern medicine is stymied and can offer no cure, the hopeless patient will often turn to the unorthodox practitioner. The trouble is, in the New Age era there are so many alternative sources available that too many turn to them when they might still be helped by the medical profession.

Some of the really way-out treatments, such as iridology, have no scientific validity whatsoever. They are mumbo-jumbo, pure and simple. To think that inspecting the eye will reveal illness in vital organs and other parts of the body is purely wishful thinking. This practice belongs in carnival sideshows. On second thought, it doesn't belong there, either.

Is there any harm to these alternative forms of medical treatment? Plenty. Acupuncture needles have been found to have done serious harm to patients when inserted too close to vital parts of the body. The *Toronto Star* of March 19, 1988 reported that inadequately sterilized acupuncture needles are one more vehicle for the spreading of AIDS.

And regarding AIDS, the snake-oil salesmen are still with us. The purveyors of alternative treatments are now exploiting the fear of this dread affliction by providing a variety of questionable "cures." They have established a huge industry that supplies worthless and sometimes dangerous pills and diets to the desperate sufferers of the disease.

By March of 1988 almost three hundred worthless AIDS treatments had been uncovered by health information centers. Some treatments include "aroma therapy," diluted arsenic and strychnine, the use of algae and "pond scum," and other ridiculous ideas.

The consumption of herbal medicines is a gamble, because many of them do not fall under government control as do other drugs. Some herbs contain powerful drugs in quantities which are not labeled. Some deaths have been reported as the result of drinking herbal teas.

These particular problems are just a few of those that arise when so many individuals get hooked by the dispensers of quick cures by exotic methods. And the sad fact is that so many of these individuals are of advanced age and can least afford the money they throw away on the quacks who take advantage of them. Because older people are more likely to be ill and require treatment, they are easy targets for useless therapies.

These shady practices have been with us for a long time, but with the expansion of irrationalism in the New Age they have multiplied like rabbits. Unlike the magician who entertains people by pulling a rabbit out of his hat, the quack practitioner robs them by promising what he can't deliver.

*   *   *

One would not think that astrology would be included in the New Age movement. After all, it has been with us for three thousand years. But the advent of Astrogate—the revelation that President Reagan and Mrs. Reagan rely on this dubious pseudoscience—has propelled astrology to the forefront of today's paranormal practices.

Former White House chief of staff Donald Regan, in his recent kiss-and-tell book on Reagan activities, told an astonished public that Nancy Reagan regularly consulted her favorite astrologer for advice on setting the president's schedule. And apparently Mr. Reagan was prone to heed this advice.

The media had a field day with these revelations. Every television talk show worth its weight in nonsense showcased at least one astrologer on one or more of its programs. Some even had two or three astrologers on at a time. Sometimes there was even the odd skeptic participant, ostensibly to lend some semblance of balance.

The newspapers jumped on the bandwagon, running critical articles that poked fun at the Reagans for following the advice of an astrologer. There were even some sarcastic editorials on the subject. Consider the irony of this approach by the newspapers, when you remember that they continue to run their horoscope columns.

The ultimate question we must pose after being subjected to all the hype and publicity surrounding the Reagon-astro revelations is: Does the president believe in this nonsense, and if so, how strongly?

In an interview in the *Washington Post* on July 13, 1980, Reagan admitted that he consulted astrologer Carroll Righter's column every day. Aquarian Reagan told him, "I believe you'll find that 80 percent of the people in New York's Hall of Fame are Aquarians."

That same year, syndicated astrologer Joyce Jillson claimed that she had been paid by the Reagan campaign to draw up horoscopes for eight prospective vice-presidential candidates. She claims that she recommended George Bush because, as a Gemini, he would be the most compatible match for the Aquarian Reagan. The Republican party denied this, of course.

At a question-and-answer session with reporters shortly after the White House astrology story broke, Mr. Reagan was asked flat out: "Do you believe in it [astrology]?" He answered, "I've not tied my life by it, but I won't answer the question the other way because I don't know enough about it to say is there something to it or not."

This answer by the president of the United States will probably be enough of an endorsement to give most astrologers a tremendous boost—to their egos and to their bank accounts.

The fact that astrology derives its roots from an era when the earth was considered to be the center of the universe, and is therefore based on a foundation of false premises, has made little difference in recent centuries. It has gone through several cycles of popularity over the ages. With the advent of channeling, crystals, and all the other trappings of the New Age, astrology appeared to be going into one of its somnolent periods. But the publicity generated by the latest flap has caused the rubber duck to surface yet again.

It is no great surprise, really, to have a head of state indulge in occult practices. Astrologers, hundreds of years ago, catered exclusively to kings, queens, and emperors. It has only been in relatively recent times that commoners have been allowed to benefit from the doubtful and dubious delights dished out by the dispensers of cosmic wisdom.

As a proud Canadian I lay claim to having had a national leader who dabbled in the occult long before Ronald Reagan. Indeed, he not only dabbled, he wallowed in it.

William Lyon Mackenzie King was prime minister of Canada for twenty-one years—a record he still holds. He must have been doing something right to maintain his position. But he had a hidden agenda that the public never could have dreamed of. He died in 1950, and when his secret diaries were publicized in 1979 it was revealed that he had regularly attended séances with spirit mediums while in office. He claimed to have been in regular contact with his dead mother, and even with his faithful canine companion after it had passed away. He was regularly guided by various superstitious beliefs.

Whether all this was responsible for the decisions he made as a politician is hard to say. Nor will we ever know how many of Reagan's decisions were founded on rational thought and how many were based on the positions of the heavenly bodies.

The Channelers

Channelers, or spirit mediums, would not be among us if there were not millions of people who wished to believe in them. And this desire springs from a more basic need to believe in an afterlife.

The promise of an existence after death is central to many religions. It is a source of sustenance to much of humankind. And it is a matter of faith. This faith should be respected. A nonbeliever does not have the right to criticize or downgrade those who hold such ideas.

The belief is that somehow a soul or spirit leaves the body at the point of death and enters another dimension, another plane of existence. For centuries this belief has given people comfort, often when they needed it most. Comfort for the dying and comfort for those left behind. Comfort based on faith.

But when certain elements of our society claim to contact discarnate spirits, they are leaving faith and theology behind— they are encroaching on the territory of science. And when they do that, they must answer to the challenge of science: Where is the evidence?

This is why skeptics—and I like to think of myself as one—take strong exception to the activities of so-called channelers who benefit from the misplaced beliefs of the gullible among us.

There are many, of course, who challenge the concept that there *is* a spirit thát survives bodily death. These people, in my opinion, deserve the same respect for their belief as do those with faith in the hereafter.

The noted scientist Isaac Asimov makes a strong case for his opinion in *Science and the Paranormal,* edited by George O. Abell and Barry Singer (1981). He draws an analogy between the human body and an intricately built model castle, constructed out of thousands of tiny bricks. The structure has all the details of a regular castle, with towers, crenellations, portcullises, and so on. He writes:

> Now imagine some giant hand coming down and tumbling all the bricks out of which the castle is built, reducing everything to a formless heap. All the bricks are still there, with not one missing. All the bricks, without exception, are still intact and undamaged. But where is the castle?
>
> The castle existed only in the arrangement of the bricks and when the arrangement is destroyed the castle is gone. Nor is the castle anywhere else. It has no existence of its own. The castle was created out of nothing as the bricks were arranged and it vanished into nothing when the bricks were disarranged.
>
> The molecules of my body, after my conception, added other molecules and arranged the whole into more and more complex form, and into a unique fashion, not quite like the arrangement in any other living thing that ever lived. In the process, I developed, little by little, into a conscious something I call "I" that exists only as the arrangement. When the arrangement is lost forever, as it will be when I die, the "I" will be lost forever, too.

Now, this is the personal opinion of one man. And to attempt to accept that opinion would be shattering to many people. Still, the logic in it should be considered, and, at least, respected.

The belief in discarnate spirits, in apparitions of the dead, has been with us for thousands of years. But the modern spiritualist movement dates only from the middle of the nineteenth century. This brought us, for the first time, the spirit medium who claimed to actually make contact with those who left this earthly plane.

The first of the spirit mediums were two young women, Margaret and Kate Fox, who began cracking their toe joints, and snapping their big toes against solid objects, back in 1848. Ridiculous, but true. These two enterprising girls lived with their parents in the hamlet of Hydesville, in upstate New York. They found that by secretly employing this strange practice they could catch the attention of their parents, then their neighbors, and finally America and Europe.

The strange knocking sounds, which seemed to emanate from nowhere, were interpreted as being messages from unseen spirits. The Fox sisters didn't discourage that notion. In fact, they devised a code, where the knocks would answer questions through a series of numbered signals.

It seems that this was the foundation for the idea that humans could make contact with departed souls from the "other side."

The Fox sisters, as they grew older, developed a baffling presentation of "spiritual" effects, and they hit the lecture circuit. They became world-famous. Their program was spooky, but it was designed for entertainment; and it became a model for many others to follow. Their earliest presentations consisted mostly of a demonstration of spirit rappings, followed by a lecture by a well-known newspaper editor, Eliah Wilkinson Capron, who helped promote their early performances. But then, the Fox sisters, under more capable management, developed the act into a more commercial proposition. They presented levitations, ghostly apparitions, and other tricks of the trade.

It was their mysterious rappings, however, and the séances they held, that established their reputation. They traveled worldwide, holding séances for credulous scientists, even for royalty. There's no doubt that the Fox sisters should be credited, or blamed, for kicking off the spiritual movement that flourishes to this day.

Strangely, this movement proliferated in spite of the fact that Margaret Fox, in her later years, made a public admission that the whole thing was a fraud. Her written confession was published in the *New York World,* on October 21, 1888, exactly one hundred years ago, and it created a sensation.

I suppose it would be equivalent to Uri Geller reserving space in the *New York Times* and writing, "Sorry, folks, it was all a scam. All these years I've been bending keys and forks and spoons and nails with my hands when I distracted your attention. Did I make the compass needles move through the power of my mind, as I always claimed? No way. I had this dinky little magnet hidden in various places on my person, and when I leaned close enough to the compass, bingo! the needle turned. Hey, did you see the looks on the faces of the TV hosts when I pulled that stunt? And how about the way I duplicated drawings that people had previously done? I couldn't even begin to tell you how many different methods I used to secretly secure that info. But, psychically speaking, folks, you've been had. And the funny thing is, even though my tricks have already been exposed and explained by people like James Randi and others, most people still don't believe I'm a fake. Well, believe it, folks, believe it."

The public confession of Margaret Fox Kane, which was her name at the time, was a little lengthy, but you might find a few excerpts from it quite interesting:

> I think it is about time that the truth of this miserable subject "Spiritualism" should be brought out. It is now widespread all over the world, and unless it is put down soon it will do great evil. I was the first in the field and I have the right to expose it.

My sister Katie and myself were very young children when this horrible deception began. . . . We were very mischievous children and we wanted to terrify our dear mother, who was a very good woman and very easily frightened. At night, when we went to bed, we used to tie an apple to a string and move the string up and down, causing the apple to bump on the floor . . . My mother listened to this for a time. She did not understand it and did not suspect us of being capable of a trick because we were so young.

At last she could stand it no longer, and she called the neighbors in and told them about it. It was this that set us to discover the means of making the raps. . . . All the people around, as I have said, were called in to witness these manifestations. . . .

My sister Katie was the first one to discover that by swishing her fingers she could produce a certain noise with the knuckles and joints, and that the same effect could be made with the toes. . . . No one suspected us of any trick because we were such young children. We were led on by my sister [Leah] purposely and by my mother unintentionally. We often heard her say, "Is this a disembodied spirit that has taken possession of my dear children?"

Margaret went on to tell how her older sister Leah took the two girls to Rochester to give exhibitions with their mysterious rappings, and to charge money for these appearances. That is where it all began.

She then exposed the exact method used to produce the rappings:

Like most perplexing things when once made clear, it is astonishing how easily it is done. The rappings are simply the result of a perfect control of the muscles of the leg below the knee which govern the tendons of the foot and allow action of the toe and ankle bones that are not commonly known. . . . With control of the muscles of the foot the toes may be brought down to the floor without any movement that is perceptible to the eye. The whole foot, in fact, can be made to give rappings by the use only of muscles below the knee. This, then, is the simple explanation of the whole method of the knocks and raps. . . .

> . . . I have seen so much miserable deception that I am willing to assist in any way and to positively state that Spiritualism is a fraud of the worst description. I do so before my God, and my idea is to expose it. I despised it. I never want to lay eyes on Spiritualists again. . .
>
> . . . I trust that this statement, coming solemnly from me, the first and most successful in this deception, will break the force of the rapid growth of Spiritualism and prove that it is all a fraud, a hypocrisy and a delusion.

Any reader who is interested in reading the published confession in full can find it in the comprehensive *A Skeptic's Handbook of Parapsychology,* edited by Paul Kurtz (1985).

As we are now well aware, far from Margaret Fox's hope that her confession would inhibit belief in spiritualism, it has mushroomed into the huge growth industry we are now witnessing. Her condemnation of the practice, her references to fraud and deception one hundred years ago, could be applied, word for word, today.

When the statement was published, the skeptics, who had long criticized the hanky panky involved, had their chance to crow "I told you so." Apparently, they were vindicated. But, Margaret's confession didn't make much difference to a believing public. The Fox sisters had established a new religion. And it refused to go away.

Spirit mediums (now known as channelers) sprang up all over the place. Suddenly, the opportunists came out of the woodwork. Everywhere, spirits (now known as entities) spoke to their loved ones through these charlatans. But, more than that, they were causing very strange physical things to happen.

If you visited a medium, you would usually take part in a séance. The medium would go into a trance. The lights would be lowered, the room darkened. If skeptics reading this have a question about the need to dim the lights, please be patient. Shirley MacLaine will explain the reasons for this practice later.

The attendees at a séance usually sat around a table with the medium, and everyone held hands. After the room was darkened, strange things would begin to happen. Often an apparition would gradually appear. The voice of a summoned-up entity would fill the room. The ghost would fade away. A large "spirit trumpet" would be seen floating in the air. Invisible bells would ring. The participants would feel a ghostly breeze on the backs of their necks. "Ectoplasm" would sometimes emerge from the body orifices of the medium. All in all, a harrowing and not-to-be-forgotten experience for the believer.

These magical effects were, of course, part and parcel of the average medium's stock-in-trade. The methods used were fairly simple, but the effect on the audience was powerful, particularly in that technologically less-sophisticated era.

The "ghost effect" was accomplished by first obtaining several yards of very fine white silk veiling. It was treated with a recipe of different solutions, including a form of luminous paint. After various other treatments and washings it was ready to go. When exposed to light, and then exhibited in a darkened room, it would appear as a soft luminous, ghostly vapor—just the thing to scare the wits out of a credulous group.

How to make the ghosts gradually appear, and ultimately vanish? In the early days the medium would sit inside what was called a "spirit cabinet"—a three-walled structure with a curtain in front. The chairs of the participants would be drawn up in a semicircle around the cabinet. The cabinet, it was explained, was a chamber where the psychic energies would be condensed. However, it was actually a "backstage" area where the medium could prepare the various effects to be presented.

Once inside the cabinet, the medium would don the veiling, then slowly emerge from the cabinet at the appropriate time. The withdrawal could be done in various ways. An effective method was to slip out of the veiled covering and let it drop slowly to the floor, then simply drag it back into the cabinet. The effect was that the apparition was dematerializing, just fading away.

The spirit trumpets and other objects that seemed to be floating in space were usually controlled by what was known in the trade as "reaching rods," which were simple extension rods; they were painted black and invisible in a semi-dark room.

The ectoplasm, which was supposed to be an other-worldly substance, was usually a thin, gauzelike material, concealed by the medium and then seemingly produced from the most unlikely bodily locations.

All these conjuring shenanigans had a powerful effect when performed years ago by what are called "physical mediums." Then gradually the "mental mediums" began to take over. And why not? The others, with their fairly transparent tricks, were beginning to be exposed. Magician Harry Houdini, for one, was making a career out of investigating and airing their precious secrets. The publicity that ensued perhaps didn't make much of an impression on the true believers, but there was enough to make things uncomfortable.

Why go to all the trouble to stage this hocus pocus and to risk discovery and ridicule? All a medium had to do was go into a trance (who would know if it was faked or real?) and pretend to speak for an entity who had temporarily taken over his body. What could be simpler?

If you were able to speak with a fairly plausible-sounding foreign accent of some kind, all the better. And if you were articulate and could talk up a storm, better still. If you could put on a good demonstration, the chances of your being exposed as a fake were almost nil. There were no secret props to conceal, no tricky physical techiques to learn.

Yes, you could be challenged and asked to prove you were authentic. But why bother? Could anyone prove you were *not* authentic? So the mental medium became a going concern and thrived for years.

This isn't to say that the physical medium hasn't survived at all. As M. Lamar Keene, a self-confessed fraudulent medium, described in his book, *The Psychic Mafia* (1976), such psychic resorts as Camp Chesterfield in Indiana and Camp Silver Belle in Pennsylvania were havens for the trumpet-levitating mediums. Indeed, Keene was one himself. These camps attracted the die-hard true believers who could be impressed with any kind of chicanery.

Reading Keene's book, one finds it incredible how easily the innocents are taken in by the simplest forms of deception. For example, a small personal item like a credit card is purloined from someone's handbag and at a later date tossed over the person's head from the rear, to land in front of her. She is convinced that the article has "apported" from another dimension.

Another stunt was to have the subject sit in a chair in a completely dark room. She would then levitate, with her chair, until she could almost touch the ceiling, and then slowly return to the floor. She would be completely overwhelmed by this *spiritual* experience. It wasn't too difficult for the two husky men dressed in black, who had secretly entered the room, to slowly lift a small woman to the ceiling, and then gently deposit her chair back on the floor.

It is through miracles like these that people have their paranormal beliefs reinforced and are motivated to contribute money—often lots of money—to the nefarious schemers who still proliferate.

Of course mental mediums and channelers don't stoop to these primitive methods. They basically depend upon impressing their clients by feeding back personal information that would seem impossible for them to be aware of. The acquiring of this information is the stock-in-trade of channelers, psychic readers/advisers, and mentalist-magicians like myself. Of course the purpose of my deceptions is sheer entertainment, and I make that clear to my audiences.

There are numerous methods of acquiring information. The techniques used for ordinary citizens are different from those used for high-profile celebrities. For the everyday visitor, the channeler might secretly obtain information that the subject had innocently written down for some apparently innocuous reason. Or he might use the psychological weapon of "cold reading"—using various ways of soliciting information from the client and then feeding it back later.

For a well-known client, it is even simpler to get background information and then use it on the unsuspecting believer. Undoubtedly, channelers who have been fortunate enough to hook Shirley MacLaine as a client and booster have had little trouble securing facts about her past. Indeed, in several of her writings she relates how overwhelmed she was when told facts about herself that "nobody could have known."

Evidence for this method will be detailed further on in this narration, when I discuss the famous medium Arthur Ford.

Whether a physical medium, a mental medium, or a channeler, the phenomenon that often has the strongest effect on a client is the trance. They almost all use it, and some are very convincing. It might be interesting to find out what this apparent altered state of consciousness is about.

D. H. Rawcliffe, in his excellent book *Occult and Supernatural Phenomena* (1979), makes some observations about the "trance state." He points out that the trance can sometimes be quite genuine, and at other times, and most frequently, it is a masquerade. A genuine hysteric, through auto-suggestion (or self-hyponosis), can become "mentally dissociated," that is, temporarily separated from the immediate environment. One could call this state "a trance." Rawcliffe's judgment is that most spirit mediums faked it.

Now, if you observe a modern-day channeler very closely, carefully monitor his speech, and note his interaction with members of the audience, you will see that he is fully aware of what's going on around him—that he is acting. It's all part and parcel of the presentation.

*   *   *

In the late nineteenth century and the early twentieth century, the storefront mediums were on almost every streetcorner. The public was being ripped off from all directions. During, and just after, World War I, there was an increased demand for spirit mediums, particularly in England. Because of the heavy loss of life in that conflagration, there were countless people who were desperate to attempt a reunion with the loved ones who had been taken from them. The mediums had a bonanza.

Sir William Crookes, the eminent British chemist of the latter part of the nineteenth century, was at one time president of the prestigious Royal Society. He was a leader in his field, a rational man of science. In addition, he had great curiosity and a consuming interest in so-called psychic phenomena.

So he set out to investigate the leading mediums of his day. And he endorsed each and every one of them as being authentic. Sir William was a great scientist, but unfortunately he was not trained in the underground art of conjuring. Like many other scientists of his time, and of ours, he was unable to recognize the deception practiced by those familiar with sleight of hand—and sleight of mind.

D. D. Home was perhaps the most eminent medium of that era. To this day there are supporters of the Home legend who claim he was never exposed as a fraud. His repertoire included the standard shenanigans: table-tilting, spirit rappings, and communications from the dead. But he also had some specialties that built his reputation as a most accomplished medium.

Home could *levitate*—seemingly without the benefit of earthly support. His most famous feat during one of his séances was allegedly floating out of one third-story window, and in again through a window of an adjoining room.

Some light (unfortunately there was very little in the aforementioned rooms) is shed on this miracle by Trevor H. Hall in his book *The Enigma of Daniel Home* (1984). Hall gives hitherto unrevealed details that suggest how this act was probably accomplished. I say *probably,* because considering that all the hocus pocus was perpetrated in the dark, there were a dozen different ways he could have created the illusion.

In his concluding chapter Hall summarizes his view of Home as a medium: "I am convinced that Home's principal secret lay in his peculiar ability to influence his sitters and those with whom he came into contact." This, of course, is the principal asset of every successful psychic, medium, or channeler. And when you consider that the original story of Home's levitation was spread by his sitters, you can take the whole fable with a few grains of salt—and throw them over your left shoulder.

William Crookes was intrigued by what he had heard and decided to launch a scientific investigation of Home. He set up some experiments for the medium, which Home passed with flying colors. Crookes was impressed. He lavished praise on Home for demonstrating that there were indeed "psychic forces." The two men became great friends.

It's important to note that Crookes took the scientific approach. He didn't acknowledge the existence of spiritualism. Rather, he was taken in by every trick and attributed each event to some unknown force, which somehow satisfied his scientific conscience.

Sir William also was involved in the investigation of the famous medium Florence Cook. She was noted for the materialization of her "double," known as Katie King. As usual, Crookes was completely fooled. He vouched for the fact that the illusion was real—even claiming that he had pictures of the two taken together. Skeptics were suspicious, pointing out that the face of one of them was never shown. This minor omission didn't bother the scientist.

One of the most renowned mediums of that earlier era was Eusapia Paladino, in Italy. She was the illiterate daughter of peasant stock, who married a performing magician when she was very young. This gave her a good start in learning the art of deception. Eusapia dominated the spiritualist scene for the next twenty years.

Paladino was said to be very attractive in her younger years, which could have been an excellent source of distraction when practicing her spiritual powers for male investigators. When Cesare Lombroso, the founder of criminology, observed Paladino's performance he was won over almost immediately. Historians of spiritualism hint that it wasn't only the spiritual trickery that did the trick. Lombroso at one time observed that he believed that her phenomena were due to a re-direction of fundamental sex-energy. His endorsement ensured Eusapia's success throughout Europe.

Psychic star Uri Geller may have boned up on the methods of deception and distraction used by Eusapia Paladino. She, too, moved about restlessly during a performance, distracting the audience. She, too, dictated the conditions of her performances and would not perform unless everything was to her complete satisfaction.

Physicist Sir Oliver Lodge was also completely duped by Paladino and endorsed her. And remember, Crookes and Lodge were members of the British Society for Psychical Research, which was formed to investigate psychic claims scientifically.

Paladino was tested by some of Europe's most brilliant scientists, including Pierre and Marie Curie. They were divided in their judgments. Many declared her a fraud, but could not discover her methods. They thought it suspicious that she had to perform in near-darkness, while she claimed that the light inhibited her powers.

When Harry Houdini applied his talents to investigating spiritualists, he became their nemesis. Those he could not expose in person, he excoriated in his book *A Magician Among the Spirits* (1924), at the height of the spiritualist craze. The book created a storm among the believers. Houdini's good friend Sir Arthur Conan Doyle was so offended that he never spoke to him again. The creator of Sherlock Holmes, master of logical thinking, was, paradoxically, a leader in spiritualist circles. He had often argued with Houdini, insisting that the magician had actually dematerialized when he made his sensational escapes from handcuffs, chains, and locked cabinets. Doyle did not accept Houdini's protestations that he used natural, though extraordinary techniques. Such is the mind of the true believer.

Getting back to the subject of Eusapia Paladino, Houdini relates how his friend Joseph F. Rinn attended a séance that Paladino conducted for a group of Columbia University professors in New York. Rinn, dressed in black, was smuggled into the darkened room. He saw that Paladino kicked a table leg with her shoe to produce rapping sounds, and later placed her foot under the table leg to float the table in the air.

Houdini's most celebrated feat in the psychic field was his exposure of Mina Crandon, known as Margery the Blonde Witch of Boston. The Canadian-born wife of a Boston surgeon, Margery began flirting with the spirit world in 1923, and went on to become world famous. Her husband supported her throughout her career, asserting that she had miraculous powers.

Like other mediums, Margery was not anxious to have

Houdini attend one of her séances. However, after much negotiation he was finally allowed to sit in. The participants sat around a table, holding hands, in the accustomed style. Margery's husband was on her right, Houdini on her left.

The medium had placed a closed box containing a bell on the floor between Houdini's feet. The spirit, which would enter the room after the séance began, would be able to announce its presence by causing the bell to ring. There would be no physical contact by anyone. Hence the box was placed between Houdini's feet so that the skeptic would more or less guard it.

What Margery didn't know was that Houdini came well prepared. Before coming to the séance he had wrapped surgical tape very tightly around his right leg. Just before entering the room he removed the wrapping. This left his leg highly sensitized. He could feel the slightest touch.

When the séance began Houdini pressed his right leg against Margery's. He would be able to feel the slightest twitch of her leg muscles. Soon he felt her leg move ever so slightly as she twisted her left foot over his right. A slight pressure of her foot on the box, and the bell rang. Wonder of wonders! The spirits were speaking again.

Houdini had several classic tilts with the Blonde Witch, which finally resulted in her exposure as just another charlatan playing the part of a spirit medium.

Another celebrated American medium was the late Arthur Ford. He hit the headlines in 1929 when he claimed to have broken Houdini's secret code and brought a message from the deceased magician to his widow. Before Houdini died in 1926 he was said to have left a code phrase with his wife, Bess, which would identify any message he might send her from beyond the grave. Houdini, with his great ego, claimed that if anyone could escape from the other side it would be he. This is why a séance has been held ever since on October

31, the anniversary of his death.

These séances have been held in theaters, university auditoriums, and on radio and television. They have generated considerable publicity and have helped to keep alive the memory of the great escapologist. In addition, they have provided a vehicle for several public personalities to draw attention to themselves. In this latter respect I, too, must plead guilty.

Twice, I have attempted to bring back Harry Houdini, the hard way—audibly. Twice, I not only failed but was embarrassed by the results.

The first time was in 1981 on the stage of Massey Hall, in downtown Toronto, at a star-studded fund-raising event for ACTRA, the electronic media union in Canada. This was a Command Performance. The Governor-General of Canada was in the audience. Every big name in the Canadian entertainment world participated onstage.

Considering that the event was being held on October 31, Halloween, the anniversary of Houdini's death, I thought it would be good showbiz to conduct a séance and try to bring the old guy back.

After perpetrating a bit of mediumistic trickery to set the stage, I lit a candle, asked for the houselights to be dimmed, and called for Harry to make his presence known. Not in the usual way of "Give us a sign." No. Flushed with what I thought would be a success, I went for the whole ball of wax. I asked Houdini to speak to us directly through the public address system. I assumed, of course, that he wouldn't need a microphone.

When I, along with almost three thousand others, heard a voice coming through I could scarcely believe my ears. But that's where the embarrassment set in. It wasn't Houdini! It was the voice of Mackenzie King!

As mentioned earlier, Mackenzie King was prime minister of Canada for many years, and a very successful and respected one. It was quite a sensation, a few years after his death, when his diaries were uncovered and revealed that he had been a frequent client of spirit mediums during his term in office.

It wasn't until a few years later that I realized what had happened. And I have Shirley MacLaine to thank for restoring my peace of mind. Her constant references to reincarnation in her writings and television appearances—how one comes back in different forms—gave me the answer I had been looking for.

The people holding séances year after year, trying to get Houdini to return, are barking up the wrong tree. Sure, he'll come back. But not as Houdini. He'll return again and again—but always in another guise. He has probably come back dozens of times already, but nobody has recognized him. So there he was, as Prime Minister King, and he went unrecognized.

Then and there I decided that if I ever held another séance I would be prepared for a surprise. And it wasn't until November 1987 that it happened.

This was at a large gathering sponsored by the Ontario Skeptics organization in the ballroom of Toronto's Prince Hotel. This is one of many local organizations whose aims are similar to those of the Committee for the Scientific Investigation of Claims of the Paranormal (CSICOP). The executive council of CSICOP was also in attendance.

It was just after Halloween, and Houdini not having shown up at any of the séances held during the past week, I decided to have just one more shot at it. Once again I called for Houdini. When a voice came booming through the loudspeakers I was shocked. It was Shirley MacLaine!

For those readers who find it difficult to accept the veracity of the foregoing anecdotes, I must insist that they are true— well, partly.

The Ford claim about receiving a communication from Houdini raised a storm of controversy. First he claimed that

Houdini's widow verified it. Later she denied it. The media had a field day with the story for many months. The result, of course, was beneficial to one person—Arthur Ford. The publicity he had received was priceless. He became known as the "Houdini medium." People from all walks of life flocked to him for readings and to communicate with the departed. He became a particular favorite of the more affluent members of society.

His strongest asset was his ability to relate personal facts and incidents out of the past. But these would be facts concerning, not the client visiting him, but the dead soul he was supposedly contacting. Most of these facts and incidents had been forgotten by his clients. They reasoned therefore that he couldn't be using telepathy. If they weren't thinking of it, how could he be reading their mind? Reasoning further, there could be only one other explanation: Ford was communicating directly with the departed.

Arthur Ford, at the age of 70, once again swept the media in 1967 with a major story. The front page of the *New York Times* carried a story that was picked up worldwide. Ford had conducted the first séance to appear on television. What made the story so newsworthy was that Bishop James A. Pike had participated in the séance.

Bishop Pike was a highly controversial figure in the Episcopalian church. He had often upset the clergy by speaking out on sex, civil rights, contraception, psychoanalysis, foreign aid, and other subjects. But then he began to question theological doctrines like the Virgin Birth, the Holy Trinity, the Incarnation, the Resurrection, and the Ascension and in 1965 was forced to resign as head of the Episcopal diocese of California, although he remained a bishop. Bishop Pike had by then become a well-known public figure.

The following year his son, James, Jr., committed suicide. His body was found in a New York hotel room at a time when the bishop was living in England. Pike was overcome by grief and guilt. Had he failed his son by neglecting the boy's problems?

He soon began to perceive occult signs that his son was trying to reach him. The time of death had been estimated at between 3:00 and 3:30 A.M. Pike found two postcards on the floor of his Cambridge flat lying at the angle of about 3:30. He also found a clock that had stopped at approximately 8:20 A.M., a time when it would have been 3:20 A.M. in New York.

The bishop was now ripe for psychics and mediums. He began to consult them in England, and then in the United States. The news of Pike's interest finally reached Arthur Ford and the landmark séance taped in the studios of CFTO-TV in Toronto, Canada, followed soon afterward.

During this séance Ford purportedly made contact with Pike's son, who relayed a message to his father through the medium. There was the usual assortment of facts that "the medium could not possibly have known." The bishop was satisfied that the contact was authentic.

The aforementioned *New York Times* story included this statement by Pike: "In the context of what we know about man's psyche transcending the space-time continuum, about mystical experience, and the accumulating evidence about extrasensory perception, plus all the data about apparent communication with the deceased—not excluding the resurrection—one can say that it is the most plausible explanation to accept it as true."

This is a perfect example of how a person, any person, when overcome by grief, may gravitate to irrational, paranormal belief and may turn to a medium for consolation.

How did Arthur Ford build his reputation as a medium? How was he able to tell people things about themselves that they "could not possibly have known"? Did he actually receive messages from the deceased?

These questions were answered when Ford died at the age of seventy-five. His private papers revealed a treasure trove of information. He had extensive files on people who had attended his séances. He had an exclusive file of obituaries covering many years, which were packed with little-known facts about the deceased. When Ford traveled, he would carry a suitcase full of death notices of relatives of clients he was going to see.

An interesting sidelight to these revelations is that the followers and believers in Arthur Ford were not shaken in their loyalty to his memory. They took the standard approach of paranormalists: Yes, he did cheat when he had to, to satisfy the needs of his flock, but at other times his communications with the entities were authentic.

*   *   *

Taking a quantum leap from the spirit mediums of the past, we now have the channelers of our enlightened age—a time of advanced technology, universal education, and sophisticated communication. Make no mistake, channeling is not a fad supported by the uneducated and the ignorant. Businessmen, Wall Street stockbrokers, professionals of all varieties are now visiting and endorsing channelers. Why? One customer suggested an answer: "It's a combination of using them as a therapist to reduce anxiety and as an economist to get an idea of what the future will be." A New York public-relations director stated, "Therapists take a very long time; psychics just zap into something." Again, the quick fix. And besides, say some of these people, a psychic or channeler is cheaper than a psychologist or psychiatrist.

At this writing, the most prominent of the channelers is J. Z. Knight, the pretty blonde former cable-TV executive from the state of Washington. Having been patronized, endorsed and publicized by Shirley MacLaine did her no harm whatsoever.

Like spirit mediums of the past, Knight became the vehicle of a disembodied spirit, an entity with a personality that caught the public's imagination. That entity is now as celebrated as the medium herself—perhaps even more so.

A channeler doesn't have to make any claims of wisdom or prophetic or magical powers. The entity gets the credit. The channeler takes the cash. Margery's entity was her deceased brother, Walter. He became almost as famous as the Blonde Witch herself. At least she kept it in the family. Arthur Ford mouthed the utterings of Fletcher, who took credit for all the Fordian pronouncements.

J. Z. Knight displays a considerably greater imagination. She has dredged up Ramtha, a 35,000-year-old warrior who ostensibly lived on the mythical lost continent of Atlantis.

In an essay in the *New York Review of Books* of April 9, 1987, Martin Gardner provided a brief but enlightening biography of Ramtha, some of which he attributed to *Ramtha,* a book based on tape recordings and edited by Steven Lee Weinberg. The ancient warrior evidently had sixty-three out-of-body experiences and became "one with the wind." He is now part of an "unseen brotherhood" of superbeings who love us and hear our prayers.

God is neither good nor bad, says Ramtha (Knight). He is entirely without morals and unjudgmental. Hell and Satan are the "vile inventions" of Christianity. There is no such thing as evil. Nothing you can do, *not even murder,* is wrong. Every vile and wretched thing you do broadens your understanding. If you want to do something, regardless of what it is, it would not be wise to go against that feeling; for there is an experience awaiting you and a grand adventure that will make your life sweeter.

Gardner comments: "Suppose a man feels the need to rape and kill a child? You might expect Ramtha would invoke karma to explain how such crimes are punished, but no— he is down on karma. It no more exists than hell or Satan. Murder is not a sin to be expiated, it is a teaching experience. You never have to *pay* for anything. Why the guilt a murderer feels is not a payment, or how a deed can be called vile if there is no evil, are questions that Ramtha, at least in this book, leaves unanswered."

Ramtha's basic message, however, is direct and simple. You are God. Therefore you are capable of creating your own reality, whatever you desire it to be. This is the message that was picked up, and is now repeated endlessly by Shirley MacLaine. And to love God, says Ramtha—and Shirley— we must love ourselves. This is the basic narcissistic message of the New Age.

Ramtha has now become a full-fledged star in his own right. When Ramtha speaks, everyone listens. J. Z. Knight keeps as busy as she wishes to be, giving private readings and conducting seminars at $400 a crack. The seminar is the way to go in today's world, no matter what you're selling.

Attend a seminar conducted by this attractive channeler, and you will see her come forward in her flowing white robes, sit on a thronelike chair, go into a trance, and then deliver a message from Ramtha—in an accent that sounds a little like Zsa Zsa Gabor's. By the way, how *did* they speak in Atlantis? Wouldn't it be interesting if someone at one of these seminars asked Ramtha to speak in his native tongue? Would that person be lifted by the elbows and carried out by a couple of attendants?

Psychics and channelers, when asked when and how they discovered their fantastic powers, can usually trace the dawning of this knowledge back to some traumatic experience. Several psychics I know of have attributed their remarkable good fortune to a blow on the head. One was hit by a car. Peter Hurkos, the Dutch psychic, claimed his revelations began when he fell off a ladder onto his head.

J. Z. Knight had it a bit easier. In 1977, she says, someone playfully placed a small, ornamental pyramid on her head. Immediately she had a vision of Ramtha. She does not say how long she had to wear the pyramid, but evidently she now can dispense with it.

It occurs to me that some enterprising hat manufacturer could design a Ramtha hat, put it on the market, and clean up. There would be no shortage of retail outlets. Occult book-shops, health-food stores, Shirley MacLaine and J. Z. Knight seminars could all share in this bonanza. When not being worn, the hat could be used to keep meat fresh or to sharpen old razor blades.

Knight's high profile and her influence on the lives of her followers concerns Reginald Alev, executive director of the Cult Awareness Network in Chicago. She advises people, says Alev, to move from their city homes to a more rural life. And people take her advice. This can and does have the effect of breaking up families. Anyone who has heard "psychics" give such advice on radio and television call-in shows can attest to the seriousness with which it is taken.

For example, when Ramtha predicted floods and earth-quakes, he recommended that people move to higher ground, particularly to the mountains of the Pacific Northwest. Well, according to the *New York Times* of November 11, 1986, more than a thousand people moved to the Yelm region of Washington State, Knight's bailiwick.

Consider the following letter from Gita, one of J. Z.'s disciples from Down Under, to Ramtha fans back home:

> I am writing this letter from the Ramtha Intensive Seattle, Nov. 14th 1987. . . . This letter is not to create fear in the Altered Ego but to create the opportunity to become sovereign and

independent and to reach mastery and freedom. I am paraphrasing Ramtha's teachings using his own words.

. . . There are choices we must make in the next two weeks if we are to survive. . . . Can you conceive of living without money, banks, credit cards, fossil fuels. . . . Come into alignment with nature. FIND YOUR LAND. It doesn't matter how it is. If you love it, it will love you back. It will grow for you. . . .

Save and store your water. Put up food stores immediately. You *must* get your food stores immediately. . . . The earth is in the throes of great changes. Volcanoes are going off to clean the sea. The power will be more awesome than we have ever known. . . . Strong and wondrous things will awaken us. There will be a warming up of the whole earth. Crops will fail. . . . There will be a melting of the ice caps in the next four years.

. . . There will be a violent reaction from Nature in all cities. It is not well to be living where there is a population density. . . . You will not be able to walk outside in the sun. You will have to go underground.

. . . Gold will not always be available. Purchase your gold as soon as you can whatever the cost. . . .

Ramtha will send the runners to protect us. . . . Embrace everything with courage. Love the earthquakes and the volcanoes, the rising of the water and the great storms. GO TO A SAFE PLACE. BUY LAND. BUY GOLD. STORE WATER. STORE FOOD. STORE CLOTHING. *Take advantage of NOW.* GO FOR IT.

Sell homes. Buy land. Store up for a hasty retreat. Also do it so you cannot be discovered if you walk away.

The letter goes on and on and winds up with, "All that I have said will unfold over the next four years. I LOVE YOU RAMTHA. I am simply the scribe for Ramtha. I can only wish you to hear and act."

This is typical of the message being spread by J. Z. Knight. Many take it seriously, and react to it. Just contemplate the disruption and the misery it can produce.

Knight's teachings are spread not only by her disciples and her seminars. Audio and video tapes have become a powerful communications tool, and she uses them to spread Ramtha's wisdom. A woman on a "20/20" television show in 1987 told of how her husband had deserted her, to move closer to J. Z. Knight, after viewing one of her tapes.

On the same program, Steven Bakker, a former Knight employee, had a revealing story to tell. It seems that one day by sheer chance he discovered J. Z. secretly practicing Ramtha's gestures and speech—and without bothering to go into a trance.

Do you find all this hard to believe? Would anyone in his right mind really believe the advice of an imaginary 35,000-year-old man? Listen to Shirley MacLaine in her book *Dancing in the Light* (1985): "One [spirit guide] was more profound than any of the others. His name was Ramtha. . . . My relationship with Ramtha was deep. . . . The mention of his name brought up feelings that I couldn't control and touched me so deeply it almost frightened me." She goes on to write about the accuracies of Ramtha's predictions for her future. "He specified the areas of my growth that needed more work. . . . He spoke of the vitamins I needed . . . and even gave me his evaluation of the script I was reading. . . . What I learned from Ramtha would fill another book."

Omni magazine has a regular column titled "First Word" that appears on the first inside page. This page usually carries an essay by a prominent person, often a respected scientist. The essayist in the March 1988 issue was none other than J. Z. Knight. Knight points out that several surveys have established that more people than ever believe in psychic phenomena and paranormal experiences. This is not news. She also informs us that people are turning away from science and that they are "turning toward the spiritual in hopes of understanding what science has failed to answer." That, too, cannot be disputed.

The tragedy is, however, that people are turning in the wrong direction. When they place their hopes, their trust, and their money in the hands of channelers, when they put their trust in Ramtha and other so-called "entities," they are relying on false gods. When they sacrifice reason for "their own realities" they are abandoning their responsibilities.

Knight goes on, in an attempt to justify the role of the channeler:

> The channeled teachers are inspired by the spirit of God and provide a means to understanding one's own relationship with God. Channeling, the phenomenon, is simply a method an individual can use to understand more of the spiritual knowledge that pertains to his or her relationship with God. Although the delivery is bizarre to conservative America, channeling can become the norm for people who have been visited by dead relatives, and as a result experience God as a warm, all-loving deity rather than a judgmental one.
>
> This understanding is entwined with the acknowledgement that God is inside each individual and that everyone is divine. This outrageous realization creates a human being who no longer echoes the truths, dogmas and social consciousness of others but starts listening to his or her own opinions. In other words, these individuals begin living their lives according to what feels right. Americans are therefore extracting an expanded awareness of their own truth from channeling.

Which boils down to "Do your own thing."

Knight tries to distance herself from the trance mediums of the past: "A channel should not be confused with a trance medium. A medium mimics the voice of the entity that he or she hears, and can interpret messages only within his or her limited knowledge. The channeled teachers are inspired by the spirit of God and provide a means to understanding one's own relationship with God."

This is obvious nonsense. A medium is a channeler is a medium is a channeler. They both operate the same way. They both claim to carry a message from a departed soul. They take advantage of the confused, the bereaved, and the insecure in our society. No amount of gobbledygook can change that *reality*.

J. Z. Knight was given this page in *Omni* to spread her message to the huge "science-oriented" readership of this publication. It's a sad commentary on *Omni*'s editorial integrity.

Another channeler in this spiritual calling is Jack Pursel, a former insurance adjuster, who has now insured himself for a more substantial income and who has likely adjusted to the better life. His disembodied spirit communicant is "Lazaris," who has never been physical; he's an "original entity," untainted by earthly failings.

Lazaris's specialty is medical advice. His ministrations are far more beneficial than those of your everyday faith healer, coming from the astral plane where knowledge is boundless. No longer is it necessary for humanity to suffer from lower back pain. Lazaris's directions to the sufferer, as expressed in one of his seminars (yes, he too holds seminars) are simple and direct: "Release it." That should do it.

Pursel is another channeler who has benefited from the publicity generated by his relationship with Shirley MacLaine. In her book *It's All in the Playing* Shirley writes approvingly of Pursel, but saves most of her praise for the entity Lazaris.

She describes Pursel as a quiet, affable, unassuming man who enjoys beauty and good food, which he and Shirley often enjoy together. She also describes Pursel's first encounter with Lazaris. No, he did not receive a blow on the head, nor was he hit by a car, or struck by lightning. He was in deep meditation when Lazaris first came to him. "At first," writes Shirley, "Jack was uncomfortable and perplexed about what had happened to him, but in time his close friends assured him that the information from Lazaris was beneficial and loving."

Apparently, that was enough. Pursel evidently decided that he had been selected to share Lazaris's "beneficial and loving" information with the rest of mankind. So, naturally, he conducted seminars, recruited clients, and took all the other necessary commercial steps one is compelled to in order to "share."

Shirley tells of having problems with ABC-TV during the making of her TV movie *Out On a Limb*. She called her friendly channeler, Pursel, for some advice on how to handle the situation.

Pursel didn't waste any time going into a trance, allowing Lazaris to take over. Shirley explains that Pursel often channels on the telephone for his clients. Such are the miracles of modern technology. One wonders if the entities are having difficulty adjusting to all these state-of-the-art, new-fangled inventions.

Shirley fills two pages describing her stimulating conversation with Lazaris and closes with: "I hung up. Talking to a disembodied spiritual entity, even on the telephone, was no longer novel to me."

Jack Pursel is considered one of the favorites of the California New Age set. MacLaine, however, gives him a minimum of space in her writings compared with what is reserved for her apparent favorite, Kevin Ryerson.

She introduces him in her first metaphysical book, *Out On a Limb* (1983). Ryerson, an avid reader of occult literature in his youth, laid the groundwork for his future activities by studying at the Edgar Cayce Institute in Virginia Beach. What got him started as a channeler? Well, the story is that whenever he meditated, the spiritual entities made physical contact with him.

Ryerson is a personable, intelligent and articulate man who speaks effortlessly on paranormal subjects. There's no doubt he made quite an impression on MacLaine—her endorsement brought him into the vanguard of the top channelers, as it did others.

His principal entity is Tom McPherson, who was an Irish pickpocket in Elizabethan England—during a former life, that is. When Tom speaks, Kevin's voice assumes an Irish brogue. Ryerson played himself in the movie based on the book *Out On a Limb*. Whatever entities he brought in also played themselves. McPherson gave a magnificent performance without rehearsal. As Shirley tells us, Kevin had trouble remembering his lines, but the entities were letter perfect.

McPherson explains this later. "[It's] earth plane anxiety," he says, "When the director yells the word *action,* the aura of every person on the set goes muddy." It makes sense—to Shirley.

Ryerson first made an impression on MacLaine when he told her things about herself that "he couldn't possibly have known." This she revealed to me during my interview with her in 1985. This is a standard method of gaining the client's confidence.

A good example of this is described in *Out On a Limb,* when Ryerson tells Shirley he visualizes her on a beach shouting "I am God." Shirley is dumbfounded. It *had* happened. But Ryerson had not been there. The man is psychic!

It didn't seem to occur to her that someone else could have been there and witnessed the event—making it possible for Ryerson to pick up the story second hand.

Kevin Ryerson owes Shirley MacLaine a debt of gratitude for his current popularity and success. Her writings about him and the influence she used to cast him in her TV film have given him priceless publicity.

Another channeler who is now much in demand, but who has not received MacLaine's notice, is Penny Torres, also known as Penny Torres Rubin. She has hung on to the coattails of J. Z. Knight and Ramtha by inventing an entity with the moniker of Mafu. This spiritual character even sounds somewhat like Ramtha. Perhaps there is some distant relationship we're not aware of.

Penny is the only one in the higher echelon of channelers that I've so far had the opportunity to meet personally. As a matter of fact, we verbally slugged it out on "The Oprah Winfrey Show" of January 14, 1988 in Chicago.

How did Penny meet Mafu and get started in this game? Her story is a little different from the others. It seems that she and her husband, a police officer, were in bed one night when they saw this apparition at the foot of the bed. Apparently it was Mafu. Penny doesn't describe what Mafu looked like, but, in any case, there he was.

Now, usually when one claims to see an apparition, the ghostly figure eventually rises up and fades away. In this case, Mafu remained stationary, but the bed rose up. Yes, that's what Penny claims—the bed levitated, with her and her husband in it.

Let's consider this. Perhaps she is mistaken. Perhaps the bed remained stationary and Mafu *descended*. That would give the effect of the bed rising. Whichever way, it was a transcendental experience for Penny—not to mention the awestruck cop beside her. Awestruck is putting it mildly. On "The Oprah Winfrey Show," Penny revealed that her macho husband wet his pants.

From that moment on, Penny and Mafu, her potential mealticket, were inseparable. He followed her around like the proverbial faithful puppy, waiting to be summoned up to perform. And he didn't disappoint on this television show.

At the beginning of the program, Penny and I engaged in a slightly heated discussion. For some reason that I cannot understand, she became irate when I mildly suggested she was ripping off the public. She accused me of being fearful of what she represented. To that I replied that fear is one of the motivations, not of myself, but of her supporters. That fear is what she capitalizes on. Belief in the occult can be traced back to ancient superstitions, and superstition has always been based on fear.

Oprah jumped in and asked Penny to produce Mafu. Penny was quick to oblige. She went into a speedy trance, which probably isn't easy to do under the time exigencies of a television program. But Penny managed it beautifully. In short order Mafu emerged, speaking through Penny's lips in a strange accent—a cross between northern Turkish and southern Russian.

And what was the basic New Age message that Mafu delivered? "Love yourself. You are God."

I was a little disappointed. This was merely standard New Age gospel uttered so many times by Shirley MacLaine and all the other gurus and channelers. I was expecting something more original, more electrifying, from Mafu.

Understanding his speech was a problem for the listener: The words were clear, but the syntax was more complex than Alexander Haig's.

When Oprah asked, "Mafu, who are you?" Mafu responded, "Ask you that which be I, I be that which you are entity all things. I be what is called one who have come unto you on this day in your time to bring unto you the greatest thing there be, that which is come by knowing that you are loved . . ." and on and on and on.

An apparently shaken Oprah then asked, "Where do you come from? Why do you have an accent?" Mafu answered, "That which is called where come from I but within you within this woman, within all peoples I am one with your father that which you are. And why speak I in this mold? Because what is called within you New Age representation it created enough controversy unto that which already had been that needed to discharge what had come to create a following and thereby to hold God, and unto what is termed the understanding of that which is termed they who seek wisdom through that which I am."

Now, before going any further in my narration of this particular Oprah Winfrey show, I'd like to say this: I have great admiration for Penny Torres Rubin. It is not easy to glibly express oneself in this convoluted manner. It must have taken her many hours of painstaking rehearsals to achieve this spontaneous flexibility and scholarship.

When Oprah recovered from Mafu's answer, she said, "Okay." Pause. "What does that mean?" There was no clarification from Mafu. But I tried to explain. It's not really supposed to mean anything. The basic idea behind paranormal gobbledygook is fuzzification. The more complex a presentation the more authentic it appears to the believer.

Try reading a book on palmistry or astrology, for example. Its content is so complicated it appears almost scientific—which it is not. Also, in the case of Mafu, the tangled language sounds almost "otherworldly."

It was easy to discern that a large percentage of the studio audience were followers and supporters of the channeler. This is a common occurrence, because producers find it useful to bring in this type of audience. But that day the producers did try to provide some balance by admitting a young man whom Oprah singled out in the audience.

He stood and told how he had been hooked by a channeler who had literally brainwashed him and ruined his life over a period of three years. This type of occurence happens more often than you would expect. I can attest to this by the number of calls I receive from disturbed parents and spouses of those who have been caught in this trap.

Channelers offer recreation to the jaded members of our society who are bored with their mundane existence. Sometimes their advice does no harm—it's of the self-help variety that you can find in many cheap paperbacks, and will cost you a lot less than the fee of a channeler. But, in the worst scenario, the more suggestible and troubled members of our communities are led down the garden path by these phony channelers claiming to have direct access to the spirit world.

In the immortal words of the immortal Harry Houdini: "Anyone can talk to the dead—but the dead do not answer."

Shirley MacLaine

Shirley MacLaine, born and raised in Virginia, began her professional career as a singer and dancer on Broadway. From there she embarked on a movie career that won her several Academy Award nominations and climaxed in 1984 when she was awarded an Oscar for her brilliant performance in *Terms of Endearment.*

Since the beginning of her career in Hollywood, Shirley has been different from the average actress in that community. She was labeled "kooky" years ago—but not for the same reason she has that same tag again today.

Shirley adopted a lifestyle of her own. Her frequent travels to distant and exotic lands demonstrated a sort of rootlessness—which later, of course, provided priceless material for her writing career. Being the only female member of the infamous Hollywood Rat Pack, which included Frank Sinatra, Dean Martin, Sammy Davis, Jr., and Peter Lawford, was a source of her notoriety. The indirect link between the Rat Pack and John F. Kennedy's White House, through Peter Lawford, pushed her profile even higher, quite apart from her established reputation as a leading Hollywood personality.

For those who have followed her career, it is not surprising that she is now willing to go "out on a limb" and espouse causes that expose her to ridicule—whether she is right or wrong. Back in the early 1960s, when sexual mores weren't quite as freewheeling as they are now, she researched the world's oldest profession firsthand preparing for her role as a prostitute in the film *Irma la Douce.*

She played a few parts of this type—the prostitute with a heart of gold—including the lead in the successful musical *Sweet Charity.* And, according to Shirley's recent writings, this may have been more than a coincidence. After all, she claims to have been a prostitute in one of her past lives— or was it in more than one? What better preparation could one hope to have for such a role?

Also in the 1960s she spoke out in support of various causes, both social and political. She joined the marchers for civil rights. She spoke out against the war in Vietnam when it wasn't popular to do so, exhibiting considerable courage in the process. These activities could have endangered her film career, but she didn't let that inhibit her free spirit.

These various activities, demonstrating a serious-thinking rational-minded person, gave no hint of what was to come. Could anyone at that time have guessed that Shirley Mac-Laine, even with her reputation for kookiness, would be hooked by the occultists and go on to be a leading guru of the New Age movement?

Her career as an author began with the books *Don't Fall Off the Mountain* (paperback in 1987) and *You Can Get There From Here* (1975). In the former she described her early years in Hollywood and recounted her adventures in far-off places. *You Can Get There From Here* covered her work for the unsuccessful presidential campaign of George McGovern, during the political phase of her activities. She also wrote about the production of her documentary film on Mao's China. You might say these books were written during her premystical period.

But even in these books she has shown a propensity for

dramatization and for stretching her imagination. Some of the incidents she describes in *Don't Fall Off the Mountain* would seem highly improbable to the average reader. But this type of book is read for light entertainment. One does not ask for proof of every anecdote.

The later books, on Shirley's occult beliefs, call for a different judgment. These writings are presented as serious philosophical thoughts and are obviously designed to influence the reader. They are peppered with unbelievable anecdotes. The various claims are so outlandish that they raise an unavoidable question in the mind of anyone who is even slightly skeptical: Where is the evidence?

She attributes quotations to leading scientists, particularly Albert Einstein, without any documentation. Shirley seems to ask just one thing from her reader—the suspension of disbelief. This is an understandable request when it comes from a stage conjuror to a theater audience, but not from the author of several books that advocate a new form of religion—even though she claims to be just "sharing her views."

The first of Shirley's "mystical" books was *Out on a Limb*. In a short time it was a best-seller, and later sold millions more as a mass paperback. Shirley pulled out all the paranormal stops on this one. She hit the public with a double whammy: Not only was it a book on the occult, which can always find a hungry audience, but it was written by a high-profile, top box-office personality. She just couldn't miss. And the timing was superb. The New Age movement was in full swing. This was just the impetus it needed.

In *Out on a Limb* Shirley endorses just about every occult phenomenon under the sun. She begins by declaring her early skepticism, as do many occultists, "before I saw the light." She then goes on to describe her meeting with David, a mythical character who initiates her into the world of paranormal bunkum—apparently triumphing over her skeptical protestations.

An obligatory romantic thread is woven into the narrative. The object of Shirley's affections is described as a British member of parliament, named Gerry, who has the misfortune to be a closed-minded skeptic. You know from the beginning that it just ain't going to work out—and it doesn't. Perhaps Shirley should have foreseen this, because, as she reveals, she and Gerry had already had a troubled relationship in a former life.

From the information I've been able to gather, the afore-mentioned gentleman, in real life, was an Australian politician—not British. The name of Andrew Peacock surfaces. If the book is supposed to be based on fact, one wonders why Shirley would stray from the facts in this case. Which raises the troubling thought: Could there be other discrepancies in the narration?

In *Out on a Limb* Shirley tells of her first channeling experience with her channeler friend Kevin Ryerson. Through him she meets the entities that begin to guide her life. Tom McPherson, an Irish pickpocket out of Elizabethan England, offers humorous but useful advice. He also is prone to booze it up a bit. But Ryerson handles it well.

But it is David who exerts the most profound influence on Shirley. He takes her off to Peru, and in a moving scene— they are both immersed in a mineral pool—he informs her that everything is *energy,* that molecular properties are easier to find than the units of energy, and that the soul is an accumulation of energy units.

Shirley is so overcome by all this that she feels a tunnel opening up in her mind. She feels herself floating in space. She is "wafting" higher and higher. She looks down on the mountains and the landscape below. And attached to her soaring spirit is a silver cord that is connected to her body down below. This mythical silver cord is the stock-in-trade of occult literature. Shirley admits to having read about it, and she recycles it and passes it along to her readers with a number of other mystical teachings she has absorbed. The silver cord is analogous to the string connecting a kite to its controller. Let go, and you're in big trouble.

Shirley's account of astral travel isn't quite as convincing as Uri Geller's aircraftless flight to the beaches of Rio de Janiero. When he returned he was able to prove his story—by pouring sand out of his shoes!

Shirley touches all the paranormal bases in this book, including numerology, the occult significance of numbers. David lectures her on the Great Pyramid of Cheops. He instructs her on how the various measurements of the structure match specific distances on the earth, and how they relate to the movements of the planets.

The key word here is "match." That's the way numerology works. In the case of the pyramid, you check certain measurements, then you seek out ways of matching them to distances between other earthly or heavenly objects. There are countless ways of making these matches.

MacLaine, with her intelligence, is probably aware of this, but chooses to ignore the prosaic explanation. It does not fit into her belief system.

In December 1987 the wire services carried a UPI story out of New York that Shirley was being sued because of the publication of *Out On a Limb*. Attorney Anthony Muraski of Ann Arbor, Michigan, representing Charles Silva, claimed that her book, written in 1983, borrowed from Silva's 1977 book, *Date with the Gods*. Muraski said, according to the news story, that MacLaine knew Silva, read his book, traveled with him for three months in the Andes, and then wrote her own book.

In Silva's book, he tells of being led on out-of-body and space travels by a young woman named Rama, while Shirley wrote of the same kind of trips with someone called David.

And Muraski claimed that "David" was his client.

I don't know the current status of the suit, but I don't think it will get all the way to the Supreme Court. The following month, another news story appeared, announcing that Silva was being deported from the United States—bodily, that is—not out-of-body. It seems that the authorities discovered that he had previously pleaded guilty to a number of sex offenses—also bodily, I presume. So they toted him onto a plane and deposited him back home in Lima, Peru. Charlie would have been better off if he had kept a low profile.

In Shirley's next opus, *Dancing in the Light,* which also hit pay dirt, she continues along the same lines. She refers to her new romantic interest as Vassily Okhlopkhov-Medvedjatnikov—"Vassy" for short—a Russian filmmaker. Her problem with Vassy is different from the one she had with Gerry. He is not that taken with Shirley's philosophies and is obsessed with Satan and evil. For Shirley, there's no such thing as evil. She explains that evil is "energy flying backward." Spell "evil" backward and you get "live." There's a message there somewhere.

In this book Shirley narrates the incredible saga of her dematerializing purse. While visiting a dress shop on fashionable Rodeo Drive in Beverly Hills, she puts her purse on the floor, removes her jacket, and then covers her purse with it. There is no one else in the store except the salesgirl, who is on the phone. After the few seconds it takes Shirley to take down a suit jacket from the rack and turn back, she sees her jacket slowly collapsing onto the floor. She lifts it in horror, to find that her purse has vanished—like magic. No one else has come into the shop. There can be only one explanation: dematerialization.

The incident doesn't upset Shirley too much, except for one thing. The purse had contained tapes of a recent channeling session she had participated in. Those tapes contained invaluable advice from the "entities." Well, believe it or not, the purse shows up later on Shirley's doorstep with everything still intact—except for the tapes. No tapes.

Later, the channeler explains the whole thing to Shirley's complete satisfaction. The entities were responsible for absconding with the purse. They had confiscated the tapes because Shirley had become too dependent on the entities' advice.

Shirley MacLaine doesn't necessarily expect the reader to accept this tale. She doesn't seem to care either way. The important thing is, it is *her* reality.

In *Dancing in the Light* we are exposed to another incident that stretches credulity. Shirley is describing one of her visits to her acupuncturist, Chris Griscom, in Sante Fe, New Mexico. Chris is not your everyday acupuncturist. When she punctures you, it's not simply to relieve pain or cure your hiccups. Rather, it's to put you into fast reverse and spin you back a few lives. According to Shirley, the needles "stimulate memory patterns locked in the cellular memory of the physical body."

For Shirley MacLaine this is a much more efficient method then the archaic one of hypnotic regression.

What may have impressed Shirley about this particular acupuncturist is that Chris did not depend on her own perhaps fallible techniques, but rather inserted the needles under the direction of her own spirit guides, which were not necessarily related to Shirley's.

Chris also has developed techniques that should be a great asset to the acupuncture fraternity. She has discovered that gold needles stimulate a higher frequency than the silver variety. She also reveals that if you breathe lightly on the needles it eases the pain of memory while stimulating the process.

But, to get back to the story, Shirley lies down on the table in preparation for a treatment by Chris. She can hear birds singing outside. Flies are buzzing around the room. As Shirley tells it, "Chris stretched out her arms and directed the flies toward the open door. Whether it was the arms or the direction, they left."

Beats Raid, doesn't it?

Reincarnation is a theme that sweeps through all of Mac-Laine's books and public appearances. Her references to the many lives she has led and the certainty with which she makes these pronouncements about these lives are sometimes ludicrous. There are millions in the East whose religious faith encompasses a belief in reincarnation, but they do not have a laundry list of each past life.

Some of MacLaine's reincarnationist claims are contradictory. Children, she says, make their own choice of parents when they decide to return to the earthly plane. And yet, referring to one of her previous existences, she writes, "I was an infant lifted by an eagle and deposited with a primitive family in Africa, where I became frustrated because they were not as advanced as I." Evidently this was one instance where she was denied her reincarnational right of free choice.

Another incident takes place when Shirley is having an enlightening and, as she puts it, "ethereal" conversation with H.S., her Higher Self. She notices a tree swaying in the wind, and asks H.S. if she can possibly control the tree's movement. H.S. answers, in effect, "Go ahead, be my guest. But first you must ask the tree's permission. All nature works in harmony."

Shirley gets psychic clearance from the tree, and through H.S.'s direction, the tree's branches stop swaying and the leaves cease their rustling. Shirley writes: "Of course it could all have been an accident. But as I had already learned, there is no such thing."

I find the latter two incidents particularly interesting, because when I had a face-to-face interview with Shirley after the book was published, I asked her if she had ever experienced or witnessed psychokinesis, the power of mind over matter.

Her answer was "No."

MacLaine's next venture, after *Dancing in the Light* was published, was a five-hour television movie based on the alleged events described in *Out On a Limb*. This television special was released with great fanfare all across the continent. Artistically, it bombed. But for the great mass of MacLaine followers it was major event.

Channeler Kevin Ryerson played himself in the film. His entities, unrehearsed, also played themselves—definitely a movie first.

Shirley tells how all this was done in her latest opus *It's All in the Playing.*

There's absolutely no doubt that Shirley MacLaine is on a roll. Her career is self-perpetuating. First, she writes a book. Then she makes a movie about the book. Then she writes another book about making the movie about the first book. Look forward to a movie about this latest book, showing the circumstances under which she wrote the book in order to describe the movie which pictured the events which took place in the first book. It's like standing in a room with mirrors on all four walls.

If you have read *Out On a Limb* you'll know what *It's All in the Playing* is about without lifting the cover. Shirley again pulls out all the stops in her mystical meanderings. She describes the hazards and the many problems of filming in Peru. On one occasion the pouring rain threatened to hold up production. Everyone was quite discouraged. But Shirley had a plan. It involved a very special pair of earrings. Let her tell it in her own words.

"I went to my purse, extracted the earrings, and put them on. Immediately the squall stopped. The rain lifted, and as I peered out the window the ethereal mist returned. Within moments one of the assistants knocked on my door and said they were ready for me." Thus are miracles fashioned.

On another occasion MacLaine writes of how she and three companions caused a package of dry twigs to burst into flames by the power of their meditation. And speaking of miracles, Shirley doesn't forget to toss in a morsel about the shrine at Lourdes, helping to perpetutate the myth that miraculous cures are a daily occurrence there. The fact is that since 1858 there have been a total of only eighteen official claims of miracles at Lourdes.

The description of one of the scenes in the movie, featuring entity Tom McPherson pouring and drinking a cup of tea while blindfolded, was, to me, quite amusing. Kevin Ryerson, assuming the personality of Tom McPherson, blindfolds himself, walks to a cupboard, pulls out a mug, and pours himself a cup of tea without spilling a drop. Shirley is astonished. But then she realizes that spirits can do anything, can't they?

Surely MacLaine, who has been in show business all her life, has at some time seen a conjuror demonstrate his tricks. And surely she has, at one time or another, seen stunts accomplished while the performer is blindfolded. And is she not aware that there are literally dozens of ways to do the fake blindfold routine? Even if it's only the old down-the-nose peek? Ryerson, like so many so-called psychics, must be familiar with some of the tricks of the trade.

One of the most incredible tales that Shirley weaves in *It's All in the Playing* is the one about the magic icon. She tells of a visit from a young woman who describes a little old Russian statue of Mary holding the baby Jesus. The icon, she is told, is named Iverskaya and had been found in an old Turkish monastery on the mountain Alfone.

This young woman possesses a photograph of the icon. She tells Shirley that after surgery she had had internal bleeding that would not stop—until she placed that photo on her abdomen. The bleeding stopped overnight, she claimed, and the doctors couldn't understand it. Neither can I—unless the bleeding would have stopped anyway. Shirley, of course, didn't think of that.

The woman asks Shirley if she would be interested in seeing the photo. Shirley wasn't sure, but "some small voice within me told me it related to the unfolding of my feminine energy." Sure, why not.

When the photo is shown to MacLaine she looks at it closely. Strange. Drops of oil are oozing out of the photograph onto the frame that encloses it. What is this, she asks. Her new acquaintance patiently explains that it's holy oil. "Whenever I am in need of help or healing I ask Mary for help and she gives holy oil."

Shirley holds the photograph. It tingles in her hand. More oil oozes out. Her friend sees this as a sign that Shirley should take possession of it. Shirley goes into her bedroom and lies down with the icon on her chest. Instantly she feels a warm tingling glow through her heart. Perhaps Mary is her spiritual guide, she reasons. So she keeps the icon photo on her bedside table and mentally communicates with it every night.

Another of Shirley's spiritual contacts is a medium named Adele Tinning from San Diego. Adele is a table-tipper and has made a strong impression on Shirley. As Shirley puts it, "Adele works with a table which is, combined with her energy, imbued somehow with the ability to spell out messages." One tip signifies "yes," three tips "no," and two tips "maybe."

The table "hovers in the air and actually leans up on one leg." The implications, says Shirley, are enormous. The messages come from spirit guides who need to use the table for communication.

When she uses the expression "combined with her energy" Shirley is quite correct—but not in the way she means it (as psychic energy). The energy Adele Tinning uses to maneuver the table is *physical*.

It is difficult to believe that Shirley MacLaine has never

heard of the many exposés of the spiritualist practice of table-tipping or of the different techniques of physically controlling a table with a combination of hand and foot leverage. Here again, if she is aware of hanky panky she chooses to overlook it if the phenomenon reinforces her beliefs.

*   *   *

The television special that covered MacLaine's claimed experiences in Peru took a severe panning from the critics. An article which appeared in the January 31, 1987 issue of *The Age,* an Australian publication, is a good example.

> The American ABC television network should distribute "I survived" T-shirts to viewers who sat through five hours this week of Shirley MacLaine's odyssey to the occult under the title of her best-selling book *Out On a Limb.*
> Survivors may also wonder if Miss MacLaine is just plain out of her tree.

A headline in the January 9, 1987 issue of the *Chicago Tribune* read: "Is She Normal or Paranormal?"

Other publications were just as critical, if not more so. Criticism ranged from knocks against the quality of the movie itself to the ridiculing of MacLaine's credulity.

What the movie probably accomplished, however, was to elevate Shirley's profile and to help sell many more of her books. The books, in paperback, are now being promoted as a boxed set. I can't remember any other series by one author that has received the same degree of hype in recent years.

MacLaine is a going concern on another front. As an outgrowth of her books, her television talk-show appearances, and the television movie, she has launched a series of seminars across the United States. At the time of this writing she is threatening to expand these into Canada and Europe. To paraphrase Winston Churchill, never has a dissemination of occult gobbledygook been spread to so many by so few—in this case just one individual.

The reports from some of the competent reporters who have attended these seminars are quite explicit.

Author Laurie Nadel, in the October 1, 1987 issue of *Family Circle* magazine, describes a seminar held in a Boston hotel, with an audience of one thousand packing the grand ballroom. Bear in mind, the fee for one of these two-day seminars is three hundred dollars per person. A rapid calculation will disclose the total take.

And this is how Shirley breaks down that three-hundred-dollar fee: one hundred for mind, one hundred for body, and one hundred for spirit. She further explains that she kept the price low so that it would not discourage attendance, but high enough to discourage random gawkers.

I would analyze the cost differently, from the standpoint of the attendees: fifty dollars to see Shirley MacLaine in person, and two hundred and fifty to have their paranormal beliefs reinforced.

To get back to the content of the seminar, as described in *Family Circle,* most of the participants, Nadel writes, appear to be comfortably middle-class, in their late thirties and early forties. The majority are women.

Shirley does mention some of the media's derogatory comments on her activities, but she tells her audience that ridicule only forces her to be more articulate about her beliefs. "We are in a spiritual age, whether people make fun of it or not. This is my role this time around, to glean this information and share it."

By communicating with our Higher Self, she states, we not only can improve our self-understanding, we also can take a step toward developing our psychic abilities. She shows her audience a chart that has a line of seven colored disks running up a human spinal column and into the head. The disks represent energy centers, called "chakrahs." Mystical Eastern teachings explain that the chakrahs are psychic centers in the body.

To align the chakrahs, Shirley suggests beginning with the color red at the base of the spine and visualizing each chakrah as a colored ball of light. Visualize red for grounding with earth and balance; orange, at the groin, for creativity and sexual energy; yellow, at the solar plexus, for emotions; green, at the heart, for love; and so on.

She then asks the audience to continue their visualization: they're in a beautiful garden; they move toward a tree containing a white light; and then, "you move closer [toward the light] . . . and you allow your higher self to emerge from it. . . . This is your real self. This is the personal God you have always wanted to meet."

The May 31, 1987 issue of the *Houston Chronicle* carried an article by Jonathan Mandell of *Newsday*. Mandell covered Shirley's seminar in New York City at the Grand Hyatt Hotel. He describes an interview with Midge Costanza, executive director of Shirley MacLaine Seminars. "Shirley guides us to find the powers within ourselves," says Costanza. "I think it's what's going to save the world. She's probably the most brilliant woman in the world today—and obviously the most courageous."

Again, there were a thousand participants at the three-hundred-dollar fee. To quote Mandell, "Some exchanged stories about their past lives and how they discovered them. Others talked about their experiences with extraterrestrials. Most seem to have been involved in spiritual matters for a long time."

Everyone entering the ballroom is required to sign and hand in a sheet headed "Higher Self Seminar Guidelines." Included is an "asumption of risk" clause: "You are aware and understand that the Seminar involves a potential risk of physical and-or emotional stress or psychological injury. . . . You are responsible for your own well-being. . . ."

Shirley announces that she is going to use all the proceeds from her seminars to build a spiritual center. "Spirituality is something you should be able to invest in not only with your heart and your feelings, but with your money." [*Applause.*]

She then continues with the chakrah colors, the white light, and all the rest of the mumbo jumbo. The audience goes home happy.

The most devastating review of a Higher Self Seminar that I read was by Marlys Harris in the September 1987 issue of *Money* magazine. Harris attended a seminar held in Seattle. Why would a writer for a finance-oriented magazine attend an occult-oriented seminar by Shirley MacLaine? Harris explains:

> I had attended many high-priced seminars—on real estate, gold, hard assets, soft assets, financial planning and financial plundering. The tabs made sense to me. After all, those seminar lectures promise their audiences overnight riches or instant success on the job. But for flocks of educated people to cough up three hundred dollars each for two long days in a drafty hotel ballroom to explore their inner beings—with no prospect of making *any* money—well, this I had to see.
>
> What became clear the next morning when I scouted the decidedly unethereal Doubletree Plaza Hotel, where the seminar was to take place, was that MacLaine was tapping into a motherlode of moola.

She estimated that Shirley would be taking in close to $4 million before this tour ended.

The audience ranged in age from approximately thirty to fifty-five. Most seemed to be intelligent, well spoken, well groomed, and well off. Many *had* to be well off, says Harris, to come from as far away as New York, Miami, and Honolulu.

MacLaine's opening remarks are best described by Harris:

Of course, as MacLaine pointed out, knowing a lot about this abstruse subject can be a disadvantage. "I became so educated in metaphysics that I actually became confused," she marveled.

She wasn't kidding. It became apparent in the course of the seminar that she still only half grasped some of the ideas she had encountered in what she un-selfconsciously referred to as "my twenty years of high-level investigations and esoteric inquiries." She informed her listeners that Seattle would be a center of "New Age searching" because of "all the trees." Trees have silica, she proclaimed (actually only trace amounts, less than in the human body), and silica is a crystal that amplifies thought. Following that logic, the Sahara would be a better site, since silica is the biggest component of sand.

MacLaine later declares that the seminars "can get quite emotional," and her attendants pass out facial tissues to the audience.

Shirley, for some reason, decides to defend the fee she charges and once more divulges the breakdown: one-third each for mind, body, and spirit. Harris observes, "Some people should have got a third off because they left their minds at home."

She also points out that every person attending one of these seminars has to sign a release allowing his or her voice to be used in any subsequent audio reproduction of the session. This raises the suspicion that Shirley is readying to expand to another front: the audio and video cassette market. In other words, she will become to the spirit what Jane Fonda is to the body. An interesting concept that merits future observation.

Being a writer for a financial magazine, it's only natural that Harris should do some calculations. She reasons that MacLaine would earn about $1 million making a movie in about nine months time. Performing in a Las Vegas nightclub would bring in about $150,000 in six nights. The seminars would probably gross $4 million for seventeen weekends. "Even if her overhead amounts to half of that, the toll of labor on MacLaine and her body would be considerably less than the highkicking and song belting required of a Hollywood entertainer."

For anyone who has followed MacLaine's various talk-show interviews, it is interesting to observe that she shrugs off criticism of her beliefs and activities quite easily. She seems to ignore the various barbs tossed at her philosophically—even accepts them with some humor. This probably endears her even more to her followers.

But the report in *Money* by Marlys Harris really got to her. In an interview on "City Lights," a program presented by City TV in Toronto on September 21, 1987, she was almost vehement in her criticism of this article and its author.

This was actually one of the few honest, blunt, hard-hitting and analytical criticisms of Shirley MacLaine's crusade to capture the minds of an already gullible public. And the first time I have seen anyone even mildly hint that her motives might include a possible interest in the dollar.

Watch Shirley being interviewed by such experienced hands as Phil Donahue and Larry King. What do you see? You see a couple of kindly gentlemen, bemused, mildly questioning, not following up too harshly, holding back, just interested in producing an entertaining program that will please the viewers. Leaning too hard on the popular star would alienate them. Basically, what they are doing is giving her a platform for her wacky theories without any real challenge.

Watch these same two hosts get a politician on the program, and see the difference. MacLaine could respond to such hard questioning, and it would make for an equally entertaining, but more informative, program.

One of the most revealing programs—revealing in the sense that Shirley was more outgoing than usual in expressing her opinions—was the "Andy Barrie Show," on CFRB-Radio in Toronto, on September 15, 1987. Barrie is one of Canada's top interviewers, an old hand at the game. Furthermore, he is a magician and a skeptic with a longtime interest in the paranormal. So when MacLaine was on his show he asked questions that had a little meat on them, and he politely fenced with Shirley at times.

As I found when *I* interviewed her, she rises to the challenge and expresses herself even more boldly than usual.

Some of her priceless statements on Andy Barrie's show are included in Part Two of this book. But I would like to mention a few things that happened.

When Barrie persisted in asking about why she believed in UFOs, she included this remark in her answer: "My best answer for believing is Jimmy Carter. When I first did *Out On a Limb* he used to call me and tell me to have the courage to say this in the private sector—because he, as president, understood there were national security reasons why he couldn't shed any sunshine, so to speak, on bringing this to public attention. But that it was in fact true. . . . I have some other friends in intelligence agencies who claim they have captured some of these crafts. . . ."

This was the first hint I'd had that Shirley was acting as a proxy for a former president of the United States to bring the truth home to its citizens. In fact, this anecdote might have *some* foundation, because there is evidence that Jimmy Carter reported to a UFO organization that, in Leary, Georgia, in 1969, he sighted a UFO, claiming that it was "self-luminous" and "bright as the moon." After intensive investigation by Robert Sheaffer, vice-chairman of the UFO Subcommittee of the Committee for the Scientific Investigation of Claims of the Paranormal, it was established that what Carter had seen was the very bright planet Venus.

Andy Barrie had gently asked MacLaine if she thought she had possibly been taken in by fraudulent channelers, psychics, and others. Her answer left a frustrated interviewer unable to think of a follow-up question: "Well, of course. I believe it because I want to believe it. I believe when I'm cured by something. Whatever moves me in my heart I am going to believe. . . . If you're talking about fraud, and someone says something that moves you emotionally, what do you care?"

Another reply by MacLaine illustrated how impossible it is to carry on a logical argument with her, or with most New Agers. In pressing her usual argument that everything bad that happens is good, because it teaches us something, she told Barrie that Hitler's genocide of millions had a teaching purpose—to show what evil was—so that it would not happen again. When Barrie reminded her of what happened many years later in Cambodia, she replied, "It happened again in Asia. This other happened in Europe. We're living in different areas of the world." She then quickly changed the subject.

The people phoning in to this particular call-in show not only were the usual MacLaine supporters—almost all said things like: "Shirley, thank you so much for bringing me out of the closet" or "Shirley, it is so wonderful to hear you expressing my thoughts."

When I interviewed MacLaine, I opened by informing her of my skeptical leanings and warned her that I wouldn't spare the probing questions. She did not object. The result was a wide-ranging discussion that touched a lot of bases and elicited a lot of interesting information.

I will admit that Shirley, unlike other enthusiasts of the paranormal, can't be backed into a corner. If you challenge her on some point that she can't respond to, she will merely answer, "Well, that's my reality." So that, as they say, is that.

*　*　*

The reaction I almost always get when I speak or write about Shirley MacLaine is: "So what? What harm is there in her writing books, holding seminars, and speaking out on her spiritual values? And so what if she endorses so many kooky claims of the paranormal? She has a right to her beliefs."

No question. Her private beliefs, like anyone else's, should not be held up to criticism. But MacLaine is not a private person; she is decidedly public. And, in her high-profile position, she wields a tremendous influence, even if, as she claims, she's only "sharing." She is leading millions of people down the garden path.

By touting the virtues of belief in UFOs, in channelers, clairvoyance, telepathy, psychokenesis, the miracles of Edgar Cayce, extraterrestrial beings, the mythical lost continent of Atlantis, the fraudulent fantasies of Von Däniken, reincarnation, precognition, astral projection—all of these unproved claims—she is even more damaging than most other purveyors of the paranormal because of her prominence, her ready access to the media and the publishing industry, and her ability to market her giant seminars.

So what it comes down to is this: If the spreading of paranormal nonsense by anyone is harmful, it is just as harmful, even more so, when propagated by Shirley MacLaine.

The hazards of getting hooked by a channeler have been outlined in the second chapter. No need to expand on that. The gamble you take when visiting any "psychic adviser" is considerable.

A person who is reasonably rational and who visits a psychic just for kicks is not a concern. It is the impressionable individual who is perhaps emotionally disturbed who is the one most likely to suffer at the hands of a charlatan. I have met many people who have been completely taken in. They will swear to the authenticity of the psychic and follow his every direction.

It is clear that some of these people require professional help, either from a psychologist or a psychiatrist or, in some cases, through a family counselor. Instead they follow the guidance of someone who is untrained in the required disciplines and who is not licensed by any professional organization.

Some of the nonsensical theories endorsed and perpetuated by MacLaine are used by many cult groups in the brainwashing of their recruits. Would this not be considered harmful? The Charles Manson group and Jim Jones followed some of the same teachings. Not harmful?

The fads now being promoted by Shirley MacLaine may be causing some damage. Let me quote from the January/February 1988 newsletter of the National Council Against Health Fraud, in Loma Linda, California:

> In the March/April 1987 edition of this newsletter we speculated that the reincarnation fad could possibly lead to suicides on the part of suggestible individuals. Since then, reports of two such tragedies have come to our attention.
>
> The first appeared in a review of Shirley MacLaine's book *Out On a Limb,* which was published in *The Australian,* August 8, 1987. The reviewer states, ". . . A coroner's court in Sydney found that a young man had hacked off his own hand and repeatedly stabbed himself, dying in a pool of blood, during what he regarded as a purification ceremony prior to doing some out-of-the-body astral traveling, as vividly described in Miss MacLaine's book and depicted in the mini-series. These unpleasant events had taken place after he read Miss MacLaine's testament."
>
> The second report appeared in *Newsweek,* February 1, 1988 in connection with a story on Frederick Lenz of Malibu, California, who promotes himself as "Zen Master Rama" and conducts seminars on meditation. In addition to reports of seduction and drug use by ex-followers, it is claimed that "Donald Cole, 23, committed suicide in 1984 because he was disappointed at his progress in the program. He left a note that read, 'Bye, Rama, see you next time.'" This obviously was a reference to his expectation that he would emerge in a new, reincarnated life in the future.
>
> These reports give evidence to the fact that mystical beliefs can be dangerous to suggestible people, especially when promoted vigorously by charismatic personalities. Surely, it is unrealistic to expect that true believers (or charlatans) will ever stop selling

psychic notions, but there is a very important ethical question for the mass media to confront. Should they continue to aid and abet dangerous fads by treating them as entertainment or public interest stories. It is doubtful that the reincarnation fad would have ever reached its present proportions without the publicity television has given it.

Well, let's be realistic. Television will not go away. And neither will the appetite of the television producers to present a personality, whether MacLaine or someone else, who has a story which will titillate the viewer—whether that story has the potential to be harmful to some viewers or not. The bottom line is—how will it improve the ratings?

Shirley MacLaine's constant repetition of the "I am God" slogan helps sell the idea that the individual can do no wrong. To some people it can condone any sort of self-centered and self-fulfilling action. This concept can lead to great harm when it occupies the minds of certain types of individuals. In my opinion, it is one of the great potential dangers of the MacLaine campaign.

Another example of the effect MacLaine and others like her can have on some people is that of the telephone caller on the "Larry King Live" television show on CNN, on September 17, 1987, when Shirley was a guest. A man called in to complain about his family being completely "blown apart" by the kind of thinking she espouses.

"My wife," he said, "in a time of depression went to a psychic healer and was told that in a past life I had murdered her and run off with her teen-aged daughter. I've not seen her in two years. I think she was looking for a crutch to avoid dealing with the realities of life—thinking things would be better the next time around. I think there's a certain group of people that can be damaged irreparably by this type of thought."

"Looking for a crutch to avoid dealing with the realities

of life" is one of the main reasons, in my opinion, that so many follow Shirley MacLaine, collect her books, and attend her seminars.

Trying to fight this trend is really a losing battle. But, if the garbage keeps piling up, we must still try to keep carting it away.

PART TWO
The "Teachings"

Philosophical "Teachings"
The Worldly Wisdom of Shirley MacLaine

"To be intelligent is to be open-minded." ("The Phil Donahue Show," Sept. 9, 1985)

The IQ controversy has been raging for many years. I have read numerous books and articles on the subject, but have never heard or read anything linking intelligence to open-mindedness.

*   *   *

Shirley pronounced that the reason she is happy with herself is because she has "looked inward" and realized she is "a very successful spiritual being." ("The Phil Donahue Show," Sept. 9, 1985)

Here Shirley expresses one of the principal tenets of the New Age movement—looking inward, being self-centered.

*   *   *

Shirley observed that "democratic idealism seemed to be no longer possible because people who were part of the democratic way of life were apparently more concerned with serving their own interests." She asserted that this contradicts the fundamental tenet of democracy, which is "the well-being of the majority." (Out on a Limb, p. 6-7)

There seems to be a departure here from the previous statement. If there is one thing that MacLaine and the New Age movement espouse, it is self-interest.

*   *   *

"I have my perceptions and my reality, and it's made me a very happy person, and you can take it or leave it." ("The Phil Donahue Show," Sept. 9, 1985)

This is the definitive argument of the New Agers. I have encountered it many times. When backed against the wall in a debate they will bring the argument to a conclusion in this manner. With this statement Shirley closes the discussion by closing her mind—and belies her claim to be open-minded.

*   *   *

"That's my reality. So no one can say whether my reality is correct or not." (Interview with the author, Sept. 16, 1985)

Shirley said this after I challenged a particularly unscientific pronouncement she had made about quantum mechanics.

Again, she asserts the *positiveness* of her own reality. How can one argue with this type of non-reasoning? It allows Shirley to make any kind of outrageous statement and then close the door on it. Throughout my interview with MacLaine she used this maneuver whenever I questioned one of the unbelievable claims she made in her books, such as the episode in which she set down her purse in a Hollywood dress shop, only to have it dematerialize and vanish.

Would it be reasonable to substitute the word "imagination" for "reality?"

*   *   *

"The question of the bizarreness of this material seems to be in direct ratio to the closed-mindedness or open-mindedness that another person might have for a reality they don't understand." ("Andy Barrie Show," CFRB-Radio, Toronto, Sept. 15, 1987)

This was in answer to a question about why rational people find Shirley's beliefs bizarre. It is, of course, obvious to her that if one doesn't understand some of her flakey theories, one is automatically closed-minded.

*   *   *

"I'm more interested in getting at the truth, rather than condemning the people who are lying." ("Andy Barrie Show," CFRB-Radio, Toronto, Sept. 15, 1987)

Yes, I will agree that the truth is accessible if you get to it. If it weren't, I suppose you wouldn't be able to get to it. Shirley maintains that we should seek truths by overlooking untruths. The problem is that scoundrels often obscure the truth, and people will accept their lies.

Her method of finding the truth is unique. "Ask and ye shall receive." Think of all the man-hours wasted over the decades as science searches for the truth the hard way.

*   *   *

Shirley presents the view that ". . . a love affair, a death, a lost job, or a disease" are all experiences that "we choose to have" so that we may be educated through them, because to Shirley "that is what life is about: learning." (Dancing in the Light, p. 12)

Note the words *we choose*. Shirley maintains that everything in which we are involved is of our own choosing. She would have us believe that we choose to be ill and even to die. Yes, there are a few cases in which we might choose death, but is *learning* the reason for that choice? And where and when would we benefit from that learning? Oh, of course— in the next life.

At least Shirley now answers the big question, the question that philosophers have been wrestling with for centuries: What is life all about? It's about learning. But learning what? Learning about astrology, UFOs, abductions by little green men, and the pronouncements of fraudulent channelers?

Shirley has learned a lot in the past few years, by her own admission. But remember the philosophy of the computer operator: Garbage in, garbage out.

*   *   *

"The purpose of living is to clear the soul's conflict." (Dancing in the Light, p. 313)

Correction. Living is not for learning—it is to clear the soul's conflict.

*   *   *

Shirley observed that if "excessive materialistic greed moti-
vates a trancechanneler," he or she won't be "free of static,"
and the communication will be unreliable and distorted. (It's
All in the Playing, p. 21)

Shirley is trying to justify the acceptance of (moderate) payment for trance channeling hocus-pocus. After all, channelers are rendering a service; how else could we get in touch with the departed? A direct line to the other side is certainly preferable to waiting for the unannounced appearance of an apparition.

*   *   *

"I remember an experience I had once. I call it an expe-
rience and not a dream, even though it happened when I
was asleep, because it felt more real than a dream." (Out
On a Limb, p. 3)

What was it, an experience or a dream? Perhaps it was the experience of dreaming? Or maybe just a dreamlike experience? Was it an actual experience that you later dreamt about? Or a precognitive dream of a future experience? Or maybe your memory of the experience happened in a dream, and the dreamlike experience hadn't really happened except in your dream of the memory? Or maybe . . . ?

*   *   *

"I had always trusted what a friend of mine described as
my built-in 'bullshit detector'—that inbred sense of skepti-
cism." (Out on a Limb, p. 18)

For Shirley MacLaine to call herself a skeptic is like calling Mahatma Gandhi a warmonger. It is not out of the ordinary for paranormalists to label themselves skeptics—but it is grotesque. Those who do not call themselves skeptics usually state that they started out as skeptics. Somewhere, evidently, they fell off the straight and narrow. But Shirley does not renounce her skepticism. She manages to straddle the fence.

*   *   *

"I was a healthy skeptic. And still am a healthy skeptic." ("Larry King Live," TV show, Sept. 17, 1987)

Shirley reaffirms her skepticism. She also reaffirms her physical condition.

*   *   *

Shirley states the importance "of taking care to refrain from being so skeptical that one automatically shuts out challenging ideas and new perceptions." (Out On a Limb, p. 18)

So, *that's* the secret of skepticism: Learn to regulate it; just be a little skeptical; don't overdo, or you will close your mind to the great ideas and the teachings of the gurus of gobbledygook. This is what Shirley had begun to learn from the channeler Kevin Ryerson, who *"would come to be one of the telephones in my life." (Out On a Limb, p. 185)*

*   *   *

"No. I project a bubble of light around the plane. I project light straight down the aisle—and in my visualization I visual-

ize the plane as a perfectly balanced aerodynamic craft that will not get in trouble." ("Larry King Live," TV show, Sept. 10, 1985)

This was Shirley's response to the question, "If you're in a plane bouncing around in bad weather, you don't get upset?" I am including the quotation above in this book as a public service. I have observed many a nailbiter in an agitated aircraft, including myself—so, start practicing your bubble-projection, everyone.

*   *   *

"I'm not proselytizing—I'm sharing." (Interview with the author, Sept. 16, 1985)

To proselytize is to convert or attempt to convert someone from one belief to another. Can someone who spreads her beliefs by writing books, conducting seminars, making movies, going on countless television talk shows, and planning to build a spiritual center really claim that she is not proselytizing?

Let's look at the definition of the word "sharing." To share is to apportion something, to divide and distribute. True, Shirley is distributing something. But when you do it for a price, it's called "selling," isn't it?

*   *   *

Shirley stated that "studio executives, bank presidents, journalists, actors and actresses, musicians, writers, househusbands and housewives" all frequented spiritual channeling sessions. She added, "No one questioned the validity of the process anymore." They merely attempted to understand the information transmitted by the mediums. This included "past-life infor-

mation, psychological information, dietary information, medical and scientific information: information about Atlantis, Lemuria, the creation of the cosmos, extraterrestrials . . . everything one could think of to ask." (Out On a Limb, p. 359)

The first sentence of this paragraph is an accurate, and disturbing, indication of the hold that occultist beliefs have over a cross-section of North America's population. Note the reference to the lack of questioning "the validity of the process."

Also, note the reference to "medical" information. The dispensing of medical advice by so-called psychics, channelers, or other charlatans is an ongoing menace that should not be disregarded. There are two ways in which this kind of advice can be harmful. First, people who kowtow to the authority of the psychic adviser will often reject proper treatment by a licensed physician. Second, many are overcome with fear when the adviser informs them of some hidden ailment of which they are not aware.

How often I have seen the look of panic in the eyes of an elderly woman when a psychic tells her to check out her right lung, or that her kidneys will give her trouble, or whatever. People frequently tell me how disturbed they were by the revelations of psychics; the psychological trauma in these cases can be quite damaging.

*   *   *

"Some of their relationships and long friendships eventually foundered because their spiritual beliefs and values could not be shared and they could not abide the cynical and intellectual limitations of the past." (Out On a Limb, p. 360)

This is a reference to the same people who became drawn in to the channelers' net. This statement says a lot, and what it tells us, in an oblique way, is very true. Many a friendship, and many a family, have been destroyed because one of the members became hooked by a psychic or channeler. It is interesting to note the phrase, "they could not abide the cynical and intellectual limitations of the past." This perhaps opens a small window into the thinking process of Shirley MacLaine's mind. She equates "cynical" with "skeptical." I find this quite common among defenders of the paranormal, and don't believe it is simply a question of semantics—it is quite deliberate. Shirley also equates "intellectual limitations" with "rational thinking." This, of course, is not stated, but the meaning is clear—at least to anyone who takes the trouble to analyze some of MacLaine's ramblings.

*   *   *

Shirley writes of referring those who wanted to read about spiritualism to the books of Edgar Cayce, Jane Roberts, and Ruth Montgomery. (Dancing in the Light, p. 16)

This is another example of Shirley's virtue of "sharing." She is sharing the invaluable advice offered by a man who was commercially built into a myth and exploited after his death; by a woman who created an imaginary psychic character; and by another woman who wrote books containing the most nonsensical claptrap imaginable.

*   *   *

". . . we are not victims of the world we see. We are victims of the way we see the world. In truth, there are no victims. There is only self-perception and self-realization." (Dancing in the Light, pp. 121-122)

Shirley, have you heard of the Holocaust?

*   *   *

"To me, understanding spiritual principles is identical to understanding scientific principles." (Dancing in the Light, p. 420)

Not only is this statement not profound, it is ridiculous.

*   *   *

"It's a concept that's too difficult to simplify in the little time that we have." ("The Phil Donahue Show," Sept. 14, 1987)

After Shirley had stated that we are responsible for everything and that we create our own reality, Donahue asked, "You are saying there's no such thing as an accident, nothing in the universe that cannot be controlled?" She responded with the above cop-out. She has repeatedly proclaimed that we create our own reality, but has never taken the time (or has never been able) to explain exactly what she means. The New Agers, indeed all occultists, thrive on the complex and the abstract. If you challenge them or try to give natural explanations for their weird theories, you are accused of being simplistic. If it's complex it is difficult to understand. If it's difficult to understand, it is more profound—to the believer.

*   *   *

". . . it was a built-in opportunity to peer into the illusion that peers into the illusion that peers into the illusion—I couldn't resist it." ("Canada-AM," TV show, Sept. 15, 1987)

This is what Shirley said when she was asked why she wrote a book *(It's All in the Playing)* about a television mini-series that was based on a book *(Out on a Limb)*.

This is a new formula which, as I see it, is just the beginning. Now Shirley can make a film about the book she wrote to describe the making of the film that described the other book. It can continue *ad infinitum*. And she can keep rolling along on the talk shows, flogging the latest movie or book, as the case may be. I can visualize a gray-haired Shirley MacLaine, wearing thick, metal-rimmed glasses, sitting in a rocking chair, regaling a stooped Phil Donahue with anecdotes about her latest book (or was it a movie?), while a bemused studio audience mumbles to itself in assent, "I am God, I am God."

*   *   *

Shirley suggested that the concepts she is exploring are "innovative for Western culture." She likened her ideas to Newton's theory of gravity and Galileo's saying that "maybe all the planets revolved around the moon." ("Larry King Live," TV show, Sept. 17, 1987)

Shirley modestly places herself in good company. And it's instructive to learn that Galileo said that maybe the planets revolve around the *moon*. Has Shirley revised scientific history?

*   *   *

"I'm not sure that there's any such thing as a mistake. I think every decision we make in our lives is a decision we want to make in order to learn from it." ("Andy Barrie Show," CFRB-Radio, Toronto, Sept. 15, 1987)

This would mean that when you make an idiotic financial decision that wipes you out, you've done it with the best of intentions—so that you would learn from it. When an ill-suited couple gets married and ends up divorced after a stormy and miserable relationship, they've done it for their own good—to learn?

True, sometimes we learn from making wrong decisions. But do we make wrong decisions *in order* to learn?

*   *   *

Shirley remarked that she doesn't consider herself to be "particularly literary" or a "really good writer," but does allow that she is "a very fine thinker." She believes her talent lies in translating her thoughts to written words "in a simple way that's translatable to an audience that doesn't consider themselves to be intellectuals." ("Larry King Live," TV show, Sept. 17, 1987)

I appreciate Shirley's self-effacing qualities, but with her many years of experience in show business, surely she knows she should never put down her audience. Does she really believe she is writing strictly for dummies? After all, *I* read her books. I even read them more than once. And it wasn't easy.

*   *   *

"It's not really bizarre. . . . Some people don't want to accept those responsibilities and therefore can't blame anyone else— that's why they call it bizarre." ("Canada-AM," TV show, Sept. 15, 1987)

This was in response to the understatement, "Some people find what you're saying a bit bizarre. . . . What makes it difficult for some people to accept is the notion that we're responsible for our destinies."

Shirley isn't quite accurate. Rational-thinking people do not find her pronouncements bizarre (among other pejorative terms) for the reason she states, but rather because of her total acceptance and endorsement of just about every cockamamie paranormal and pseudoscientific theory under the sun. Or is it the moon?

*   *   *

"It's based on the point of view that everyone's point of view is right for them." (Publishers Weekly, Sept. 25, 1987, 75)

Referring to the New Age movement, Shirley reaffirms her support of its self-serving philosophy. Everyone's point of view is right for them regardless of how it affects others.

*   *   *

"Sometimes people use pain to feel alive. Pain is a perception, not a reality." (Time magazine, Dec. 7, 1987, 67)

This absurd observation was made, according to *Time,* to a woman at one of MacLaine's seminars who complained that she had suffered chronic physical pain since childhood. It would be interesting to know whether Shirley's wisdom had a positive effect on this woman.

Shirley might be interested to know that people generally do not experience perception and reality as a dichotomy— perception is usually based on reality. And if pain is just a perception, then a lot of researchers are wasting a lot of time and money studying a non-reality.

*   *   *

"Doctors . . . are so confused with this disease they don't know what to do. Maybe this is the purposeful good of the disease, by the way. . . . There's a purposeful good to everything. . ." ("City Lights Show," City TV, Toronto, Sept. 21, 1987)

This was Shirley's response to a question about AIDS.

Is she trying to say that the AIDS epidemic can be beneficial in that it confuses the medical profession? It seems to translate that way. There's something to be said for altruism, but I'd like to see her try to convince an AIDS sufferer that there's a "purposeful good" in his affliction.

*   *   *

"I wondered whether coming into the Aquarian Age (as the astrologers and astronomers called it) also meant that we were coming into an age of Love and Light." (Out On a Limb, p. 357)

As the *astronomers* called it? I searched feverishly through the book for a reference as to which astronomers are alluded to. No luck.

*   *   *

Shirley writes of being "fascinated" with the possible veracity of psychics and trance mediums. "Wherever the information came from didn't matter as much to me as the sense it made. Maybe it was a psychic's subconscious talking; maybe they were just good actors. But even if that were true, the morality of their message was unmistakable." (Out On a Limb, p. 112)

This is exactly the same philosophy expressed by Marilyn Ferguson, author of the New Age bible, *The Aquarian Conspiracy* on "The Oprah Winfrey Show" of September 18, 1987:

> I think that phenomena like channeling and the effect of crystals . . . is not the main point of what the New Age is about . . . the same thing with so-called past life experiences. They can be extremely helpful to people, *and we don't have to know whether they were authentic or not.* (Emphasis added)

Whatever happened to truth?

*   *   *

"We invent God, and everybody has invented God in the image they'd like to see it." (Interview with the author, Sept. 16, 1985)

Shirley and her New Age adherents go even further by claiming, "I am God."

*   *   *

"Touch your divine mass purpose." (*Los Angeles Times,* July 20, 1987)

Isn't this getting a little personal?

*   *   *

The creative technology of perceiving alternative realities is a quantum leap in the progress of mankind." (*It's All in the Playing*, p. 335)

If you say so, Shirley.

*   *   *

"The whole point of this, and why I found such peace in it and such total responsibility for my own destiny, is that I understand that I'm creating everything in my life." (Interview with the author, Sept. 16, 1985)

This probably summarizes Shirley MacLaine's philosophy. Right or wrong, it has helped her—if she is sincere in her assertions.

*   *   *

Metaphysical "Teachings"
The Real Truths About the Paranormal

"Tom McPherson, one of the entities that Kevin channels, knew intimate details about me and my life which no other human being on earth knew." (Dancing in the Light, p. 80)

This is the classic "hook" used by so-called psychics to ensnare their victims. The methods used to obtain this information are numerous; some have been outlined elsewhere in this book.

When the psychic makes a hit, telling the subject something about her that he "couldn't possibly have known," he makes a lasting impression. This usually ensures her coming back for more and, also, passing along news of this miracle to her friends and acquaintances, thus helping to build the psychic's clientele. And can you imagine a more illustrious backer than Shirley MacLaine?

*　　*　　*

"You know when you get shivers when someone says something to you—that's your higher self telling you it's true . . ." ("The Phil Donahue Show," Sept. 9, 1985)

This might be a useful yardstick for establishing the truth, but only in southern climes. In the northern latitudes, where shivering is much more·common, it would not be very reliable.

*   *   *

Shirley believes that "energy alignment between planets" allows for a personal connection with the "moment of energy" present at birth. She declared: "Every time I go to some of those people (astrologers) they all say the same thing about me—and they're always right." ("Larry King Live," TV show, Sept. 10, 1985)

This was Shirley's response in reply to a question regarding her belief in astrology.

Her explanation of that pseudoscience is rather muddy. But so are its claims. It isn't surprising that astrologers all say the same thing about her, and that they're *always* right. (Though I question that last phrase, since Shirley has been known to exaggerate a bit.)

In any event, when a celebrity visits a fortune-teller (also known as an astrologer, psychic, channeler, tea-leaf reader, palmist, etc.) that operator usually knows enough about the subject to give a seemingly accurate reading.

*   *   *

Shirley writes, "Talismans work in human understanding because we ascribe magic to them." She also noted that "magic works wonders" and its loss is the "denial of unlimited possibility." (It's All in the Playing, p. 243)

A talisman is a good-luck charm believed to serve as protection against demons. The use of talismans reached a peak during the Middle Ages.

The talisman does sometimes work as a good luck charm, but only because of self-fulfilling aspirations. If a student carries a talisman into an exam session, she may do well as a result of the confidence it inspires. The same for an athlete in competition. However, it is not the magic wrought by the talisman that accomplishes this—it is the thought processes of the carrier that are responsible. This can be proved by secretly removing the good luck charm from the owner's possession without her knowledge, before the event. She will carry on with the same confidence and get the same results. It's not the magic, it's the thought of magic.

MacLaine's statement is actually contradictory. She is correct when she writes that talismans work because we ascribe magic to them. But then she states that magic works wonders. She can't have it both ways.

The last sentence is very revealing. It says a lot about the philosophy of those who believe in the occult. They hang on to their beliefs because they desire the never-never land of "unlimited possibility." Unfortunately, there *are* limits to possibilities. But the occultist, ridden with anxieties, requires instant solutions to all problems and cannot cope with uncertainties.

*   *   *

Shirley writes of "often" experiencing precognition, and claims that the events were realized. (Out On a Limb, p. 88)

Now, here's the kind of statement one hears often, coming from the true believer and even from the mild believer. And, when directed to me, it is usually followed by the question, "Can you explain it?"

Yes and no. (How's that for a New Age reply?)

First, this particular claim is packed with generalities.

There are no references to specific cases. In cases where specifics are mentioned, it would require documentation for evidence. Seldom have I seen documentation for these types of claims. And where there *is* documentation, there is something else to be taken into account, namely, *coincidence* (a dirty word to occultists).

Still, we must look at these things from the viewpoint of statistics and probabilities. What are the chances of such a thing happening, and how often does it happen?

The believer tends to ascribe a paranormal explanation to every one of these strange and puzzling occurrences. Why not? It's a quick fix, an instant and easy answer. And it helps to reinforce an already predetermined mindset.

*   *   *

"Definitely, you're an old soul . . . there's an open-minded left brain intellectuality in you that speaks to the profound humanity in everybody, and that's an old soul." ("Larry King Live," TV show, Sept. 17, 1987)

This was in response to Larry's question about reincarnation: "Was I here before?"

Here Shirley refers again to her favorite subject, the left and the right brain. I find it just a little difficult to accept this explanation for Larry's reincarnation. Shirley, however, was firm and confident in her reply.

*   *   *

"Yes, that's what I've learned. And sometimes when we feel this tremendous familiarity for a certain species of animal or a pet, and we think we've known them before, we probably have." ("The Phil Donahue Show," Sept. 9, 1985)

In response to, "Do animals go through reincarnation?"

This can be very reassuring to a pet owner. But one wonders how the animal might feel about returning to the former master.

*   *   *

"People come back as people, but not as animals. But animals come back as different animals." ("The Phil Donahue Show," Sept. 9, 1985)

Again on the subject of reincarnation, but this time she sets herself up as an authority on the transmigration of souls.

Reincarnation implies that death has been vanquished, that the soul reappears inside different bodily forms throughout eternity. It is a very appealing notion and, to some, a necessary source of hope and comfort. As a religious belief or a philosophical idea it is difficult to dispute. I have no quarrel with a belief based on faith, but when Shirley MacLaine goes into great detail about past lives, hers and others, without proof of any kind, it becomes ludicrous.

The way in which transmigration occurs has been a subject of dispute for centuries. Some occult authorities claim the human soul can return in the body of an animal, or even in a metal. The Hebrew Kabalah claims that the wicked return as animals. The ancient Egyptians believed that the soul must go through a cycle of three thousand years, reposing in one animal after another until it can return as a human. The prevailing European view today, for those who faithfully believe in reincarnation, is that the human soul cannot dwell in an animal.

But Shirley does not equivocate. She has probably received the message from her favorite channeler. She is quite definite. Let us not question.

*   *   *

"I think we've all had an experience that makes us palpate to some other dimension. . ." ("Larry King Live," TV show, Sept. 17, 1987)

This was Shirley's answer to the question, "Why do you think so many people believe in what you're saying [about reincarnation]?"

A fairly accurate reply. When those who are disposed to superstitious and occultist beliefs have a strange experience, they tend to attribute it to ESP, reincarnation, or whatever. However, I disagree with the assumption that we can *all* "palpate to some other dimension." There are still a few rational-thinking individuals among us who do not palpate too readily.

*   *   *

Shirley writes of "pure channels" and "channels who have so much emotional static of their own that the teachings from 'the other side' are quite garbled and even inaccurate." She has encountered both and describes them as equally "fascinating." (It's All in the Playing, p. 16)

What a beautiful cop-out. What Shirley is telling us is that some psychics give poor readings. But of course it is not because they haven't polished up on their questionable trade, but rather because the messages are disturbed by "emotional static."

You know what it's like when you don't set the fine-tuning accurately on your television set—you get a garbled and inaccurate picture. And that's exactly what happens to the poor channeler. He has knocked off his fine-tuning with "emotional static" and screwed up the reception from the other side. Amateurish and unforgivable.

Shirley finds this fascinating. I find it wackily hilarious.

* * *

"The UFO contacts were coming up in connection with spiritual searching because the callers understood that the basis of the knowledge the extraterrestrials were bringing was both a scientific and a spiritual knowledge of the God-force." (It's All in the Playing, p. 68)

She is commenting on the telephone calls coming in on her many talk-show appearances. Many of these callers were citing their flying-saucer sightings and experiences. Shirley is attempting to explain her version of the reasons for these experiences.

* * *

Shirley explains that extraterrestrials are very advanced scientifically. She believes they have "learned to harness the unseen energies in the cosmos and use them in a beneficial manner." This, MacLaine writes, explains high-speed space travel, dematerialization and rematerialization, as well as how extraterrestrials can defy linear time frames. She states the reason for their obscurity is that ". . . mankind would tend to revere them as gods and abdicate personal responsibility for their own human growth." (It's All in the Playing, p. 68)

There you have it! For years we have been puzzled by the UFO phenomenon. Yes, there have been prosaic explanations for some of the sightings, for some of the personal experiences. But the basic questions have remained un-answered.

How could the flying saucers get from there to here? How could they cover those astronomical distances in a reason-able time? How would they sometimes seem to vanish, and then reappear in a different location? And lastly, why have they been skulking around our planet for so many years without going public?

Sure, they do land in the odd swamp or cow pasture—but why not on the White House lawn, or, more dramatically, on top of the Empire State Building, *a la* King Kong?

Well, Shirley has just laid it all out. If you missed it in all of those scientific studies, don't worry—it's all explained right here.

*   *   *

Shirley said that she became "very interested" in UFOs, but could not explain why. She added: "I've had two sightings, but I can't say they've really had an effect on me. I saw the craft, and I saw other craft coming on, and I took it very naturally." (Interview with the author, Sept. 16, 1985)

Many prominent people have stated their views on UFOs; many support the phenomenon. But, when asked if they have ever sighted one the usual answer is "No." Shirley is an exception in more ways than one. She took it "naturally," which reveals something of her tendency to accept without question anything in the realm of the supernatural. Unless pure fantasy has taken over.

Can anyone imagine an adult of reasonable intelligence seeing extraterrestrial space ships and just calmly accepting the scene?

When I asked, "You accepted that they were from another

world?" Shirley answered, "Uh huh. I knew it was true."

Shirley, you were just putting me on—I hope.

*   *   *

Shirley observed that the trappings (tarot cards, tea leaves, etc.) were only "tools that enabled the psychic to attune to a higher level of awareness." She stated that this "awareness" is available to everyone through contact with the "all-knowing" higher self. (It's All in the Playing, p. 282)

A lot of psychics might not agree with the assessment in the first part of this statement. They would claim that the fall of the cards, the position of the leaves, and the lines of the palm do divine the past, present, and future of the hapless subject.

Shirley's theory that these are merely tools for reaching a higher level of awareness has as much evidence to support it as do the claims of the psychics. That is, none.

The truth is that all these mystical methods, including crystal-ball gazing, state-of-the-art psychic computer readouts, and the composition of astrological charts, have as much validity as reading the entrails of a dead chicken.

These *are* tools, but they are not used for the purpose that Shirley claims. They are used to lend an air of mysticism to a reading, to make a stronger impression on the subject.

In addition, they give the psychic other advantages. As the tarot reader lays down the cards, he gives himself time to think and to concoct more wisdoms, more forecasts and more banalities. When the palmist holds your hand, she, too, has time to stall while mentally polishing her predictions. Each reader learns to make the best use of his or her specialty for the greatest effect on the gullible visitor.

Good presentation is everything. A top-notch channeler

will not simply begin speaking for the entity he is supposed to be bringing in. I have seen some second-rate channelers who don't even impress some of the would-be believers. The better ones will pretend to go into a trance in a very convincing manner. They will then, also convincingly, change their voices and their accents. It's showbiz, folks. Do it right.

When Shirley writes that we can all contact our "higher selves," she is merely echoing the line of all the purveyors of the paranormal, that we all have ESP potential, and so on.

*   *   *

Shirley writes of channelers' being "profoundly shocked" when listening to tape recordings of their sessions. She remarked that "Often there was no agreement at all between the beliefs of the channeler and the beliefs of the spiritual entity. But always there was an agreement that the entity had permission to use the body of the channeler." (It's All in the Playing, p. 18)

I, too, am profoundly shocked. It's the naiveté of Shirley MacLaine that I find difficult to accept. Does she really believe that a channeler would come out of a trance and then admit to be aware of the words that came out of his mouth while he was supposedly in the trance? That would simply blow his cover. And for the channeler to pretend to disagree with the supposed entity just makes simple common sense by reinforcing the whole charade.

It is reassuring that the entity is always given *carte blanche* to use the channeler's body. Without that permission there would be no channelers, no entities, and fewer books by Shirley MacLaine.

*   *   *

Shirley declared that there is no "difference between channeling an advanced spiritual guide and channeling your own higher self." She stressed that the higher self is "as advanced as any other guide and needs to be recognized as readily." ("Andy Barrie Show," CFRB-Radio, Toronto, Sept. 15, 1987)

This is a revolutionary concept that could put all the channelers out of business, if I read Shirley correctly. Why visit a channeler who contacts his own personal guide for you, when you can talk to yourself for free?

*   *   *

"In déjà vu you are getting an overlap of a past life experience, or you could be getting an overlap of a future life experience . . . that's what Einstein said." ("Sally Jessy Raphael," Sept. 29, 1987)

Déjà vu is one of Shirley's favorite subjects. Many paranormalists use it as an explanation for the validity of reincarnation. When MacLaine attributes it to a *future* life experience she joins a few others who break new ground—which makes her theories just a little more unbelievable than they already are.

For the enlightenment of some of my readers, and, hopefully, of Shirley MacLaine, here are a few facts about déjà vu: As we know, déjà vu is the strange sensation one gets of feeling that some circumstance has happened before, when we believe it could not have happened. Perhaps your first visit to a certain location gives you the vague feeling that you have been there before. Or perhaps it is an auditory experience. These things are usually of short duration, and quickly forgotten—unless you have leanings toward the paranormal.

In some cases this can be caused by a psychiatric disorder associated with temporal brain lesions, but this is comparatively rare. Déjà vu happens quite often to perfectly normal people, and the reasons are quite prosaic.

A strange street seems familiar? Most likely, some of the buildings resemble those you have already seen in other locations, perhaps even in a photograph. You are talking to a friend on the telephone, and she says something which you would swear she said before under similar circumstances. But you can't recall such a conversation. Not to worry. There's a good chance that it did happen, and you simply can't dredge it out of your memory, which can be quite unreliable at times.

Here you have to make your own judgment. Did you have this experience in another life—or could there simply be a blank spot or a distortion in your memory? Just read a book or two about the psychology of memory, and it will make your decision much easier.

And, by the way, Shirley, I am curious as to where Einstein made that astounding statement you refer to.

*   *   *

"I have had present déjà vu, which means, you know, when you sleep you have this imagination that you are dreaming." Shirley explains that this is a "separate reality." She added that "when you are feeling that maybe you have been somewhere before, it is possible that during the dream-state you left the body and went there." ("The Phil Donahue Show," Sept. 9, 1985)

Here is some information to add to the vast amount of literature on the dreamstate. When you dream you are not dreaming—you are imagining that you are dreaming. When your body seems to be resting comfortably in a warm bed, you are really taking that long-delayed vacation to an exotic foreign land. You are traveling thousands of miles at bargain rates. So there is something to be said for astral travel. As Woody Allen once observed, "This is not a bad way to travel, although there is usually a half-hour wait for luggage."

There may be something to Shirley's theory, however. Could it possibly account for those mornings when you wake up feeling more tired and spent than you had when you retired the previous evening? In any case, Shirley has now covered all the bases. She had already accounted for déjà vu of the past and the future; now she has taken care of the present.

*   *   *

"I've been developing that." ("The Phil Donahue Show," Sept. 9, 1985)

This was MacLaine's reply to Phil's question, "Do you believe you can see into the future?"

Up to this time Shirley seemed to be concentrating on advancing her various theories on the paranormal and expressing her beliefs in the hocus-pocus practiced by others. She had often described her own "psychic" experiences.

But in this statement she makes an outright claim of possessing psychic powers of her own.

*   *   *

Shirley claims that there have been instances where her "own psychic talent" has been utilized to tell "what happened in the past and what happened in the fuure." She declared she was "completely right," although she didn't know the people involved. ("Andy Barrie Show," CFRB-Radio, Toronto, Sept. 15, 1987)

Here, two years after the previous statement, MacLaine does not equivocate. She is no longer "developing" her powers, she is now exhibiting them. As Shirley herself might express it, this is a *quantum* leap from just being a believer. Does this mean she will soon be hanging out a shingle, *Shirley MacLaine, Channeler?* Will she open a nationwide chain of tea-leaf-reading parlors? An astrology institute? Do we have the ingredients here for a new movie, featuring Shirley the Shaman? MacLaine the Magnificent? Don't be surprised. Anything can happen when you can create your own reality.

*   *   *

"I really think we are all creating our own reality. I think I'm creating you right here. Therefore I created the medium, therefore I created the entity, because I'm creating everything." (Interview with the author, Sept. 16, 1985)

When I questioned Shirley about the authenticity of her medium, or channeler, Kevin Ryerson, she suddenly became defensive and launched into this New Age maneuver which, of course, gets her off the hook. Without a good argument in her favor she simply says that everything is in her own reality.

When I countered with a weak, "But Ryerson is a reality to me and to others," she answered, "In my dream he is. But I don't know if he's a reality to you."

Did you ever try nailing jello to the wall?

*   *   *

"I would say anybody's own higher self, anybody's own superconsciousness, can zero in on anyone else's, and when we're very, very aligned with our own superconsciousness we know everything about ourselves and everybody else." ("Andy Barrie Show," CFRB-Radio, Toronto, Sept. 15, 1987)

Shirley spills the beans. Now we know how she, and every other "psychic," operates. Just align the old superconsciousness and you're in business.

*   *   *

"I think there are times when mediums must feel the pressure to be accurate because others put so much stock in making them their guru, that they feel that pressure." (Interview with the author, Sept. 16, 1985)

This was in reply to my observation that the chicanery of many mediums and psychics has been exposed. Two glaring examples I mentioned were Arthur Ford and Uri Geller.

Ford was a world-famous medium who sat for some of the most high-profile people of his day. His reputation was untarnished until he died; when his survivors went through his personal effects they discovered files of information he had secretly gathered on many of the people who came to him.

His supporters saw no problem with this. He had to do this, they reasoned, in order to maintain the faith of the believers—so that they would not feel let down on the days the spirits didn't come through. Or, perhaps, as Shirley might say, when there was static in the astral plane.

In the case of Geller, the superpsychic, the same reasoning applied. His flummery was exposed so many times that it is amazing that, to this day, there are literally thousands who still believe he has powers beyond that of the ordinary mortal.

Those who aren't aware of his fraud still believe in him, and his supporters pooh-pooh the exposures. Apart from a few instances when he stooped to sleight-of-hand, they say, he was the real thing on all other occasions.

Shirley has been well indoctrinated. She reads the right books and gathers information from the right people. Her pro-paranormal observations are strikingly similar to those of these sources.

*   *   *

"Way back in the backlog of evolution . . . we were creating these little beings. That's why we're still involved with nature and ecology, because all this is our creation." ("The Phil Donahue Show," Sept. 14, 1987)

In response to Phil's question, "Can we also channel with animals—cats, dogs, and so on?"

It would take a greater authority than myself to judge this learned comment on evolution.

*   *   *

"The Bible itself is a metaphysical form of writing. . . . When I began to read the Bible is when I began to form these thoughts." ("The Phil Donahue Show," Sept. 14, 1987)

This is the first time I can recall Shirley leaning on the Bible as her authority; she later mentioned its reference to voices, to channeling, to UFOs, and to apparitions.

Here she attributes her reading of the Bible as the catalyst that led to her paranormal beliefs. On other occasions she has referred to other reasons for her path to her higher self. Consistency is not one of her best qualities.

*   *   *

Shirley urged her followers to visit metaphysical and holistic bookstores. She said that in these they would find "some incredible stuff written" about holistic massage and acupuncture, as well as how diet, particularly too much alcohol and red meat, affects the ability "to get in touch with those intuitive realities." ("The Phil Donahue Show," Sept. 9, 1985)

Incredible stuff available in metaphysical bookstores? That's understating the case. But I don't think that Shirley is interpreting the term "incredible" in the same way I would.

In these bookstores, once you acclimate yourself to the haze of incense smoke, you will find a mystical mass of mumbo-jumbo that will send your senses reeling. If you can find one book with some realistic, rational, commonsensical content, you are inclined to think someone on the staff slipped up.

And you needn't go to one of these shops to find that collection of nonsense. Just wander over to the occult section of any bookstore; you'll find the shelves groaning from the weight of this type of literature. Ask the clerk to direct you to the skeptical book section and you'll see a glazed look as he racks his brain to think of where he might find even one or two such books.

When I interviewed Shirley, she maintained that she was not proselytizing. Directing the public to this type of reading material, in my opinion, comes under that heading.

As far as alcohol and red meat are concerned, I know that one affects your equilibrium and the other your cholesterol. Regarding their effect on your intuitive realities, whatever that means, I am yet to be convinced.

*   *   *

Shirley writes of having read much of Elisabeth Kubler-Ross's writings, which include "documented accounts of so many people describing the same phenomenon when they were pronounced clinically dead." (Out On a Limb, p. 173)

This is in reference to the so-called near-death experience, when the subject claims that his soul has traveled through a tunnel with a white light at the end of it or experienced other such transcendental flights, and returned to the land of the living to tell about it.

Several profitable books have been written on the subject. There have also been rational, scientific explanations of this phenomenon, but somehow, publishers have not rushed to put these explanations into print.

Kubler-Ross has devoted a lifetime to helping the dying and has written extensively on the subject. But of late she has branched off into the realm of the paranormal, for which she has been duly criticized. It is not my purpose to criticize her in this book. But when Shirley MacLaine writes about "documented accounts" it brings to mind a Kubler-Ross press conference I attended a few years ago. She made one paranormal claim after another, many of them regarding the near-death experience. After about twenty minutes of this, I asked the question that no one else seemed to have in mind: "Do you have the documentation?" the answer: "No, but I will have it."

Now, this is the answer I get from every so-called psychic or paranormalist I have ever debated. Either that or, "Yes, I have it and I'll send it to you." To date, *after many years,* not one piece of documentation has ever been sent to me.

I have written to Elisabeth Kubler-Ross since that time and received no reply. So Shirley, if you have any of the documentation, please send it to me. I'll reimburse you for the postage.

*   *   *

"Don't you think everyone has had something happen to them that they can't explain?" (Out On a Limb, p. 230)

No question. But does that mean that we must opt for the fastest, easiest explanation, which is often the paranormal one?

In this age of instant information, instant coffee, instant this, and instant that, humankind seems to need a quick fix on everything. Who has the time or inclination to look for the natural explanation for a bump-in-the-night experience? You won't find those explanations in Shirley's writings. But you will find them in the increasing volume of skeptical books now coming out. Their number is minuscule compared to those of occult literature, but they are there.

*   *   *

"Spiritual entities say they can see our vibrational light-frequencies better when electricity doesn't interfere with the medium's own eyes." (It's All in the Playing, p. 29)

Shirley uses this as a reason for turning down the lights during a channeling session. I have been collecting psychic cop-outs for many years, but this ranks as one of the winners.

For a hundred years spirit mediums have been performing their wondrous miracles in the dark. Can you blame them? How else could they produce ectoplasm (fluorescent paint-tainted gauze) from body orifices? Or float spirit trumpets (supported by extension rods) in the air?

Today, the mental medium, or channeler, doesn't really need to dim the lights—there's nothing physical to hide. But it does lend a mystical air to the performance.

Aside from that, it's Shirley's pseudoscientific explanation that really grabs me. Her imagination soars higher than the astral plane!

*   *   *

"The soul is located in the heart chakrah." ("Larry King Live," TV show, Sept. 10, 1985)

For centuries the controversy has raged—Does our human species, each and every one of us, possess a soul, a spirit, somewhere inside of us? In the 1870s scientists began to launch a search for it. Could it be found, measured, weighed?

Sir William Crookes, the renowned British chemist, was a solid supporter of the spiritualist movement. He was one of the first to make an attempt at this impossible task. He tested the solidity of an apparition which appeared to him in a gaslit room. Crookes was satisfied—science wasn't.

At the turn of century, a Dr. Duncan MacDougall attempted the weighing of souls at the Massachusetts General Hospital. He weighed dying patients just before and just after death. The good doctor declared that the soul had to be a gas, a solid, or a liquid, and could therefore be weighed. He claimed that some of his tests showed a minute weight loss; hence the soul had just left the body. The medical profession did not rush to endorse his findings.

Others have tried over the years. Scientifically speaking, no evidence has turned up as yet. It's still a matter of faith.

But where Shirley MacLaine is concerned, there is nothing but certainty. Not only is she convinced that there is a soul, but she knows exactly where it is.

So, what and where is the heart chakrah?

According to mystical Eastern teachings there are seven chakrahs, or psychic centers, in the body, ranging from the center of the forehead "the third eye" to the base of the spine. The heart chakrah is, of course, in the vicinity of that organ.

So rest easy. We now know where the soul is located.

*   *   *

"The Andes are a very feminine energy . . . all psychics are working with a feminine energy." ("Sally Jessy Raphael," Sept. 29, 1987)

Energies have gender? A new problem for science to tackle.

*   *   *

"The [etymological] derivation of the word 'disaster' is 'disastrato,' torn away from the astral. So when we're not in contact with the astral dimension we are experiencing disaster. That's how important spiritual understanding is to each one of us." ("The Phil Donahue Show," Sept. 14, 1987)

Shirley has repeated this pronouncement on several occasions.

Disastrato is an Italian word meaning "not having a (lucky) star." She throws us a curve by using a slight distortion of the meaning in order to bring in the occult "astral dimension."

*   *   *

"I'm learning to look into the future [through mind traveling] and if I want to change it, I can." ("The Phil Donahue Show," Sept. 14, 1987)

The basis of all magic is the assumption of man's power over nature. In this statement Shirley indicates that she is on a power trip—if she is sincere in her assertion.

On this same program, two years earlier, she stated that she was learning to look into the future. Evidently her progress has advanced immeasurably; she can now actually *change* the future.

*   *   *

"I've never had what I would call a really revelatory experience until comparatively recently . . . mine was a slow progression." (Interview with the author, Sept. 16, 1985)

Compare this with her statement on the Phil Donahue program seven days earlier, that she had had a déjà vu experience at the age of six.

*   *   *

Shirley presented the case of [Edgar] Cayce. She described how Cayce placed himself in a trance and dispensed medical advice. She writes that he "always used medical terminology and prescribed from what was obviously a thorough knowledge of medicine, a subject about which Cayce knew nothing." She writes that if the prescriptions "were followed accurately, they always worked." (Out On a Limb, p. 110)

Edgar Cayce died in 1945. The myth of his accomplishments is perpetuated to this day, due to the establishment of the Association for Research and Enlightenment in Virginia Beach, Virginia, which has stored reams of printed material that attribute miracles to this man.

Known as the Sleeping Prophet, while in a trance Cayce

was supposed to have helped to cure thousands who had written to him for medical advice. In addition he made numerous predictions concerning future cataclysmic world events that never did take place.

Shirley states that he had no knowledge of medicine, strengthening the fable that he was a miracle-worker. Let me quote from my book *ExtraSensory Deception*:

> Cayce's followers cite the fact that he was not a physician and had no medical training. How could he be so knowledgeable without possessing some occult powers? Overlooked is the fact that for years Cayce did a tremendous amount of reading on the subjects of osteopathy and homeopathy. In those days "home remedies" were in fashion, and he consistently recommended many of them. How would you like your friendly physician to prescribe some of the following for you: peanut-oil massage; oil of smoke; ash from the wood of a bamboo tree (for tuberculosis); bedbug juice; or fumes of apple brandy from a charred key.

The treatments always worked? Where's the documentation, Shirley? Sure, many people wrote in claiming they were helped. The ones who were not helped weren't likely to *take the trouble to write and complain.* The ones who died didn't bother to write.

"Always" is a strong word, and it shouldn't be used loosely.

*   *   *

Shirley again writes of Cayce channeling "all kinds of medical and scientific information." She stated that accuracy baffled doctors since he was without medical training. They "couldn't understand" how he was "always right." (Dancing in the Light, p. 81)

Again the same theme. And note that word "always" again. It's interesting that this particular remark was supposed to have been made by Shirley to her mother. We would then have to assume that she is quite sincere in expressing this view, which would therefore indicate that she has been well-coached by the occultists, or had gullibly digested the questionable literature on the subject—or both.

I occasionally make these references to her possible sincerity because this is a question I am always being asked when the subject is Shirley MacLaine. Many people just can't believe she can be that gullible, and question the motivations for her crusade.

*   *   *

"Hurry up and clean up the karmic debris." (*Los Angeles Times*, July 20, 1987)

Somebody should, and it's not too soon.

*   *   *

"Karma only exists because there's an emotional hook there. When the emotional hook is eliminated because you have aligned yourself with the light, you become your own vision of God." ("Andy Barrie Show," CFRB-Radio, Toronto, Sept. 15, 1987)

I'll need more time to decipher this one.

*   *   *

"Not only was my higher self creating events in this lifetime for me, but I could sometimes feel it creating other time and place experiences as well." (*It's All in the Playing*, p. 191)

Shirley, you're spreading yourself too thin.

*   *   *

"Consciousnesses interact with each other. And if you see something positive in a previously seen negative event, you can literally change the reality of it by seeing something better in it." ("Larry King Live," TV show, Sept. 10, 1985)

Does that mean that you can change an event that has already happened in the past? Can you see the possibilities in Las Vegas?

*   *   *

"When we had déjà vu experiences, perhaps we were not actually seeing something in a past/future life sense, but inadvertently shifting to a different aspect of the whole . . ." (*It's All in the Playing*, p. 189)

I'll reserve judgment until I can figure this out.

*   *   *

"When I was first told about Ramtha, a very strange soul-memory feeling came over me. As a matter of fact, the first time I heard his name I broke down and sobbed." (*Dancing in the Light*, p. 125)

No comment.

*   *   *

". . . We are experiencing physically that which we program in the consciousness, so that the body reflects what the consciousness desires . . . and your consciousness is perfect." ("Andy Barrie Show," CFRB-Radio, Toronto, Sept. 15, 1987)

Nothing is perfect, Shirley—unless you sit down and contemplate an egg.

* * *

Question: "Why don't UFOs land in big cities?"

"Because somebody would think it was a staged event, probably, there." ("Larry King Live," TV show, Sept. 10, 1985)

Well, yes. I guess the little green pointy-eared characters do have their morals, probably.

* * *

Question: "Have you found that you have become psychic?"

"Yes. Because the more attuned you are to yourself, the more you are to others . . . The more my superconsciousness opens up, the more sensitive I get to other people. . . . Right this moment, thinking about your question, I'm getting aligned with my own life. I can see my higher self. Now, as I go up more, I can see my own guardian angel. Who knows if this is real. It's my perception of what is real, and it makes me feel wonderful. That's the way I feel with reality." ("Sally Jessy Raphael," Sept. 29, 1987)

No criticism here. If Shirley and her angel are hitting it off, and she's happy—that's her reality.

*   *   *

"Consciousness changes everything. If you are angry, your car won't start." (*Money* magazine, September 1987)

Kick the tires, Shirl, kick the tires.

*   *   *

Scientific "Teachings"
The Intertwining of
Science and the Paranormal

"'For the scientist who has lived by his faith in the power of reason, the story ends like a bad dream. He has scaled the mountains of ignorance, he is about to conquer the highest peak; as he pulls himself over the final rock, he is greeted by a band of theologians who have been sitting there for centuries.'" (*Out On a Limb*, p. 361)

Though this seems to reaffirm Shirley's spiritual convictions, it was actually written by the scientist Robert Jastrow regarding the delight expressed by theologians when scientists confirmed, with the Big Bang theory, that the universe came into existence suddenly. After all, weren't they correct all along, and way ahead of science? God said, "Let there be light."

Shirley has gone to great lengths to dig up quotes from scientists who have spiritual leanings. Fair enough. However, this particular quote by Jastrow drew fire from Isaac Asimov, a scientific authority in his own right: ". . . Jastrow is implying," writes Asimov in the winter 1980/81 issue of the *Skeptical Inquirer,* "that since the Bible has all the answers—after all, the theologians have been sitting on the mountain peak for centuries—it has been a waste of time, money, and effort for astronomers to have been peering through their little spyglasses all this time."

He then goes on to demolish the arguments of the fundamentalist creationists regarding the formation of the universe and the earth. And it is not only the theologians who are sitting on Jastrow's mountain peak, says Asimov, "but a whole melange of primitive bards and medicine men."

*   *   *

Shirley speaks of science "as a system in which you can prove that which you already know." But she challenges the argument that metaphysics, which she labels as "beyond the physical," cannot be proved in "physical" terms. She believes that "maybe quantum physics will make it more possible." ("City Lights Show," City TV, Toronto, Sept. 21, 1987)

You can't prove paranormal claims in physical terms; therefore, to ask for evidence is futile. This is a standard cop-out.

Shirley brings quantum physics into almost every discussion at the proverbial drop of a hat, though I strongly doubt that her grasp of the subject will have university faculties pursuing her for a textbook on it.

*   *   *

"A teacher is just another person who inspires you to remember what you already know. So when you go into meditation you're getting into touch with that internal knowledge which is everything. We all know everything." ("Sally Jessy Raphael," Sept. 29, 1987)

I had a problem with where to place this statement. Philosophical, Metaphysical, or Scientific? It could probably fit into any of these niches. Unfortunately, there is no "Educational" chapter.

*   *   *

Shirley explained that acupuncture is the "relief of psychic pain." She went on to describe the experience: ". . . you have the impression that you are seeing scenes in front of your mind, that begin to unfold inside your own mind. I thought at first . . . it was my imagination. I am, after all, in an overimaginative business." ("Larry King Live," TV show, Sept. 10, 1985)

The ancient Chinese practice of acupuncture has gained quite a foothold in the west. Despite much controversy, many in the medical profession quietly endorse it, but mostly as an analgesic—not as a treatment for disease. The literature associated with acupunture is almost as complex and mystical as that of astrology. Shirley seems to unwittingly put her finger on an important point here. Psychologists would probably agree that her imagination has much to do with her paranormal beliefs, and with many of the experiences she recounts in her books and interviews.

*   *   *

"You are meditating, by the way, when you are depressed. Depression is a biological meditation." ("Sally Jessy Raphael," Sept. 28, 1987)

Not being a psychologist, I hesitate to comment on this seemingly profound observation. I have researched depression in several psychological textbooks but have been unable to find it defined anywhere as a biological meditation.

*   *   *

"Nothing ever dies—science tells us that—nothing ever dies, it just changes form." ("The Phil Donahue Show," Sept. 9, 1985)

One of the principles of physics tells us that all the matter and all the energy in the universe remain constant, although they can change in form. But science does not tell us that nothing ever dies.

*   *   *

"All science is looking for the explanation of God." (Interview with the author, Sept. 16, 1985)

Science searches for the secrets of the universe—it does not look for "the explanation of God."

*   *   *

"The learning process which is karma is not punitive. It simply follows the laws of science—for every effect there was a cause— so that in the human condition, karma translated as experience, all experience." (Dancing in the Light, p. 314)

Reincarnationists look on karma as a sort of cosmic report card—a way to keep track of the soul's record throughout eternity. In each succeeding life the individual is rewarded, or punished, according to his past deeds. So to say it is not punitive is inaccurate, as is illustrated, for example, by India's caste system.

Shirley's amusing effort to cite the scientific principle of cause and effect is typical of occultists. Wherever they can find a link between science and their irrational theories, they will do so. This is the phenomenon I have termed "latching on to the coattails of science" (LCS).

*   *   *

". . . as physics and mysticism claimed, consciousness was the forerunner of everything." (Dancing in the Light, p. 347)

Another example of LCS—linking physics and mysticism.

Is Shirley saying that there were living, conscious beings on earth before earthly matter was formed? Or that the rocks and mud were conscious? Or . . . what *is* she saying?

*   *   *

"This becomes a molecular discussion—this becomes a quantum physics discussion, when you look at what each human being is doing with their lives and their emotional self-realization." ("Andy Barrie Show," CFRB-Radio, Toronto, Sept. 15, 1987)

Molecular? Quantum physics? MacLaine loves to bring these two terms into her discussions. They do have a scientific flavor, even though they have nothing to do with the topic at hand.

*   *   *

"I like to share . . . the material of understanding what science is saying now, that reality is what we perceive it to be . . . that I can create myself in any way I choose, and that if I'm aligned with the molecular forces of nature I can use that alignment to achieve a balance of peace." ("Andy Barrie Show," CFRB-Radio, Toronto, Sept. 15, 1987)

Is science really saying these things? Or is Shirley Mac-Laine saying them—in the name of science?

*   *   *

"Einstein said there's no such thing as time." ("The Phil Donahue Show," Sept. 14, 1987)

Shirley quotes Albert Einstein more often than she does any other scientist. How she pulls these quotations out of the air is one of the greatest secrets of the universe that science is seeking to uncover.

In developing his general theory of relativity, Einstein had to develop a fourth dimension in his calculations. Instead of using space he used time as the fourth dimension; this became known as spacetime. These theories are, of course, very involved—but the point is: at no time did Einstein state, "There is no such thing as time."

For Shirley MacLaine, a little knowledge is a dangerous thing.

*   *   *

"They see this white light, this loving, loving energy—something they feel as unconditional love. There's been a lot of books written on that—medical, scientific books. . ." ("Larry King Live," TV show, Sept. 17, 1987)

Here she is referring to the near-death experience.
A lot of books? Well, several. Scientific books? Not really.

*   *   *

"I think everyone is looking at the world in terms of their reality. That's what quantum physics is telling us. When the observer is in the lab looking at the subatomic particle and watching it change according to the consciousness of the observer, he's creating a subatomic particle." (Interview with the author, Sept. 16, 1985)

The LCS phenomenon again.

There are certain properties of the subatomic world that science has not yet fully explained. The tiny particles that make up this subatomic world act in a way that defies common sense, but in time, as usually happens with scientific endeavor, the answers will be forthcoming.

When a pair of light particles, called photons, interact and fly off in different directions, some of their properties seem to interact. For example, the polarity of one particle seems to affect the polarity of the other even though they are far separated from each other, and traveling in opposite directions. And this interaction takes place simultaneously.

The occultists pounce on this phenomenon as being a demonstration of telepathy. There is no basis for this claim, particularly since the theory of relativity establishes that no energy or information can pass between the particles faster than the speed of light.

When measurements are taken of the action of these particles, the measurements themselves seriously affect the position, velocity, or direction of movement of the particles. The particles are affected by the measuring instruments, not by the consciousness of the scientist doing the measuring or the observing, though this "consciousness claim" is very popular with occultists.

For Shirley MacLaine to state that the observer is *creating* a subatomic particle is simply an exercise in absurdity. She will never win a Nobel prize for physics.

*　　*　　*

Shirley explains that "Photons were vibrational energy which had consciousness." She discusses how the "'consciousness' of the photon" interacts with the "consciousness of the scientific observer." This resulted in "the dancers" and "the dancing" becoming one. (Dancing in the Light, p. 338)

All right, Shirley, you've made your point—photons have consciousness. In a pig's ear.

Her reference to "dancers" and "dancing" is interesting. She obviously picked that up from one of her gurus, Gary Zukav, who wrote *The Dancing Wu Li Masters* (1979). This book is labeled as an overview of the new physics, and is one of several publications pushing the LCS movement.

The back cover of the paperback edition tells us that "Gary Zukav has written 'the Bible' for those who are curious about the mind-reeling discoveries of advanced physics, but who have no scientific background." I couldn't agree more. Because, for those who do have a scientific background the book is utter nonsense. But not to Shirley.

*   *   *

"There were times, during channeling sessions, when the energy of the entities coming through affected the electromagnetic frequencies of the electrical equipment, causing them to jam or the batteries to die. . ." (*It's All in the Playing*, p. 196)

This took place, according to Shirley, during the filming of the television epic on her book *Out On a Limb*.

Well, she should not have been surprised. When you play around with entities, you're asking for trouble. Sometimes the spirits just don't enter into the spirit of the occasion. Consider the poor unrehearsed entities with no acting experience and no knowledge of the technical intricacies of modern film production. It's difficult enough on them—one can hardly expect them not to barge around helplessly, expending their excess psychic energy, fouling up state-of-the-art equipment, and generally behaving in an undisciplined manner.

*   *   *

Shirley writes of Wilder Penfield's research: "In his opinion, the mind was not lodged in the brain. The mind had no specific center location within the body. The mind appeared to be everywhere—in muscles, tissues, cells, bones, organs." (Dancing in the Light, p. 341)

If Dr. Penfield were alive today he would more than likely have an interesting rejoinder to this statement. The problem with researching Shirley's outrageous statements is that there are no references in her books as to their origin. To plow through the writings of a scientist in search of a statement that he most likely did not make is a thankless procedure.

After many years as a practicing neurosurgeon researching the physiology of the brain, Wilder Penfield naturally had a strong curiosity concerning the possibility of a mind-brain duality. Here are just a few excerpts from his 1975 book, *The Mystery of the Mind*:

". . . the mind has no memory of its own as far as our evidence goes" (p. 82). This knocks down MacLaine's reincarnational theories about the mind or soul carrying forward memories from one life to another.

"To suppose that consciousness of the mind has localization is a failure to understand neurophysiology" (p. 109). Which means, Shirley, *no* localization—which also means not "everywhere."

". . . I believe that one should not pretend to draw a final scientific conclusion, in man's study of man, until the nature of the energy responsible for mind-action is discovered, as, in my opinion, it will be" (p. 114). In other words, the mind-brain controversy could be settled either way—so reserve judgment and do not make conclusive statements until the evidence is in.

It's highly unlikely that the man who made these statements would make the one attributed to him by Shirley MacLaine.

*   *   *

Shirley writes that "Everyone involved with spiritual progress develops their psychic capacities." She claims they can "plug into the astral energy and 'see' whatever they wish to attune to." She likened the experience of tuning into another person's "electromagnetic wavelength" to that of tuning a radio channel. (Dancing in the Light, p. 318)

Shirley is referring, of course, to extrasensory perception. She ignores the fact that after many years of research parapsychologists have yet to furnish evidence that ESP exists.

To compare the process to that of a radio would call for certain requirements. First, to transmit electromagnetic energy from the brain further than a few millimeters would require a power source of considerable wattage. This has not yet been discovered in the exploration of the brain.

Second, to "tune in" to any particular wavelength, as does a radio receiver, requires an oscillating circuit tuned to the same frequency. Again, no evidence for this in our gray matter.

Of course, this is a scientific argument, which will slide off Shirley like water off teflon. It's not *her* reality.

*   *   *

"I have the capacity to hold contradictory points of view simultaneously in my mind and not be confused by it. This is a left-brained approach." Shirley corrected herself and acknowledged that she meant a right brain approach. She went on to explain the left side of the brain controls logic, while the right side is intuitive. She spoke of trying to "balance the feminine [right] side and respect it as much as I do the masculine [left] side of my brain." ("Larry King Live," TV show, Sept. 17, 1987)

This is another of Shirley's favorite topics. She will pontificate on the left and right brain at the slightest provocation.

As a result of research that showed each side of the brain to be dominant in certain areas, the notion of being left-brained or right-brained has become a part of our pop psychology. The idea has grown that each hemisphere operates independently in its own specialized role, though further research proved that both sides work in cooperation with one another.

The paranormalists conveniently ignore these later findings and barge along, trumpeting the "scientific" facts that fit their own theories.

The May 1985 issue of *Psychology Today* magazine reported the findings of Dr. Jerry Levy. According to this University of Chicago biopsychologist, who has spent years in research on the subject, the claim that the left hemisphere controls logic and language, and the right controls creativity and intuition, is not a scientific fact. It is a myth.

The entire brain is a necessary unit. Don't leave home without it.

*   *   *

". . . The male power structure rules the world and that is why most people are right-handed." (Dancing in the Light, p. 352)

This statement isn't quite as wacky as it might seem. You see, Shirley believes that most males are motivated by the left side of the brain—ostensibly the intellectual, practical, non-emotional hemisphere. And the left brain is known to control the motor movement on the right side of the body. Logically, then, this adds up—doesn't it?

*   *   *

"In my experience [homeopathic and holistic methods to help cure AIDS] are beginning to work. There are a lot of people now . . . who are beginning to work [that is, recover from AIDS], because there is no other course for them to take, with visualization and meditation and color therapy—holistic therapies, alternative therapies—in lieu of taking drugs that destroy the immune system and the virus simultaneously." ("Larry King Live," TV show, Sept. 17, 1987)

A danger exists when people with serious illnesses give up on scientific, mainline medicine and turn in desperation to practitioners of alternative medicine, to faith healers, and quacks and charlatans. Someone who has as high a profile as Shirley MacLaine does should not encourage AIDS sufferers to use meditation and color therapy instead of following the advice of their physicians.

Certainly, science is still struggling to discover a cure for this dreadful disease; the medical profession is doing everything it can to ease the pain and suffering and to prolong life. Do occult-oriented practitioners have something better to offer—other than false hopes?

Larry King asked the logical question: "Do you know people with AIDS who have done this and gotten better?" "Oh yes," answered MacLaine, "They're there. They're being examined—they're watched." Send me the documentation, Shirley, and I'll believe it.

*   *   *

Shirley presents the argument that artistic inspiration comes from "something else." She said it's that "something else" that she's "interested in exploring." She wants to bring the "unseen reality into balance with the seen reality. Or as science would say, 'the antimatter into the world of matter,' which we can see." ("Canada-AM" TV show, Sept. 15, 1987)

It's the LCS factor again. Shirley seems to find it difficult to make a simple, nonsensical paranormal statement without hooking on an equally nonsensical pseudoscientific pronouncement.

* ˙   *   *

"When three or more people are gathered with the same intentionality in a room, the energy units are squared." ("Andy Barrie Show," CFRB-Radio, Toronto, Sept. 15, 1987)

No comment.

*   *   *

"Crystals are amplifying minerals. You have a crystal in a radio set—it amplifies the sound waves. You have a crystal in a television set—it amplifies the light waves. When you hold crystals they amplify the thought waves, the consciousness waves. I use them quite often." ("Sally Jessy Raphael," Sept. 29, 1987)

Just a few words, Shirley, from me to you, without malice, with the best of intentions, and with but one desire: to inform and educate.

Crystals, Shirley, do not amplify. To amplify is to make larger. In the case of electromagnetic waves, to increase the amplitude, in the case of sound waves, to make louder. Crystals sometimes do other things, as I explained in an earlier chapter, but they don't amplify. Trust me, Shirley.

Now, about having crystals in a radio set. Some expensive shortwave receivers do use them for stabilizing the tuning. But as far as ordinary radios are concerned, they haven't had crystals in them for over sixty years. Mind you, you might still be using a crystal set built on a breadboard in 1922, in which case I apologize for my inaccurate statement. And, oh yes, about the sound waves in the radio sets. Sorry, Shirley, there are no sound waves in radios. They are produced by the loudspeaker, outside the radio. In your case, they are produced by the earphones outside your crystal set.

Now, moving along to the television set. I hate to sound redundant, Shirley, but there are no crystals in television sets. Even in those at the Smithsonian Institute. And, of course, you know what I'm going to say next. That's right—there are no light waves in television sets.

Regarding your claim that crystals magnify thought waves—I'll have to leave that to the judgment of the reader. I don't wish to intrude on *your* field of expertise.

*   *   *

"If you understand that your relationship to relativity is not only physical but it affects your consciousness, your consciousness awareness is the science of what you perceive your reality to be." ("The Phil Donahue Show," Sept. 14, 1987)

Phil did not reply to this statement. Who can?

*   *   *

"Air . . . means life force. Every time you are breathing you are giving yourself life force. And in the energy of the air is the stimulation for all knowledge. When you breathe deeper and slower than usual you are ingesting the life force at a different intensity than usual. . ." ("Sally Jessy Raphael," Sept. 28, 1987)

Following this reasoning leaves me breathless.

* * *

"If one says audibly 'I am God,' the sound vibrations literally align the energies of the body to a higher attunement." (*Dancing in the Light*, p. 119)

It does sound scientific, doesn't it?

* * *

"With each lifetime, we are spiraling upward. Consciousness energy moves in spirals. We actually should be living in structures that are more round . . . because that would be architecture that promotes higher consciousness." ("Andy Barrie Show," CFRB-Radio, Toronto, Sept. 15, 1987)

Buckminster Fuller was ahead of his time.

* * *

"I think it (the full moon) amplifies consciousness, both negative and positive—and we can do what we want with the amplification. . ." ("Larry King Live," TV show, Sept. 17, 1987)

There are books packed with nonsense about the effects of the full moon. Here's another gem to add to the collection.

* * *

Question: "Why, if, as we know, there are many more people alive today than ever lived before, where are all the reincarnated souls coming from?"

"We haven't just lived on this planet—we have been inhabiting, and that's why we're so haunted by the stars ... the overpopulation in the world is equal to the need to balance and cleanse the energies in the world, and that's why all the souls are coming in." ("Larry King Live," TV show, Sept. 17, 1987)

I think what Shirley is trying to say is that they're coming in from all over the cosmos. With humankind trying to find a way to colonize other worlds, what a situation we're going to create! The bodies will be vacating this planet—and it will then be overpopulated with spirits. A haunting prospect.

*   *   *

"The cosmic law spirals the light." (*Los Angeles Times*, July 20, 1987)

Uh-huh.

*   *   *

"The vibrational oscillation of nature is quickening." (*Los Angeles Times*, July 20, 1987)

And so is my pulse when I read through these nonsensical statements.

*   *   *

"The energy of violence is a slower, more dense vibrational frequency than the energy of love." ("Andy Barrie Show," CFRB-Radio, Toronto, Sept. 15, 1987)

It would be enlightening to see some reference as to where the measurements were taken of these energies.

*   *   *

"When you expect something it has a vibrational frequency to it. You are exuding an energy pattern that affects the environment." ("The Phil Donahue Show," Sept. 14, 1987)

Eliminate the words "vibration" and "energy" from the paranormalists' lexicon, and they would be speechless.

*   *   *

"All time is happening at the same time." (*Los Angeles Times,* July 20, 1987)

Imagine, if Einstein were alive, what a challenge that statement would be to him.

*   *   *

Epilogue

To close this book, let me quote from Shirley MacLaine's own epilogue in her book *Dancing in the Light*:

> *"To be skeptical of all I have described is understandable."*

Selected Bibliography

Abell, George O., and Barry Singer. *Science and the Paranormal.* New York: Charles Scribner's Sons, 1981.

Bernstein, Morey. *The Search for Bridey Murphy.* New York: Doubleday & Co., 1956.

Christopher, Milbourne. *Search for the Soul.* New York: Thos. Y. Crowell, Publishers, 1979.

Ferguson, Marilyn. *The Aquarian Conspiracy.* Los Angeles: J. P. Tarcher Inc., 1980.

Gardner, Martin. *Science: Good, Bad and Bogus.* Buffalo: Prometheus Books, 1981.

Gold, Bari. *Crystal Energy.* Chicago: Contemporary Books Inc., 1987.

Gordon, Henry. *ExtraSensory Deception.* Buffalo: Prometheus Books, 1987.

Hall, Trevor H. *The Engima of Daniel Home.* Buffalo: Prometheus Books, 1984.

Keene, M. Lamar. *The Psychic Mafia.* New York: St. Martin's Press, Inc., 1976.

Kurtz, Paul. *A Skeptic's Handbook of Parapsychology.* Buffalo: Prometheus Books, 1985.

MacLaine, Shirley. *Dancing in the Light.* New York: Bantam Books, 1985.

MacLaine, Shirley. *It's All in the Playing.* New York: Bantam Books, 1987.

MacLaine, Shirley. *Out on a Limb*. New York: Bantam Books, 1983.

Penfield, Wilder. *The Mystery of the Mind*. Princeton: Princeton University Press, 1975.

Rawcliffe, D. H. *Occult and Supernatural Phenomena*. New York: Dover Publications, Inc., 1979. Originally published as *The Psychology of the Occult* by the Derricke Ridgeway Publishing Co. Ltd., 1952.

Stevenson, Ian. *Twenty Cases Suggestive of Reincarnation*. Charlottesville: University Press of Virginia, 2nd ed., 1974.

Wilson, Ian. *Mind Out of Time?* London: Victor Gollancz Ltd., 1981.